Who *Stole* My Retirement?

...and 10 ways of getting it back.

Shawn T. Williams

Shawn Williams is the founder and President of:

Solomon Group, LLC.
Office: 832-387-4323
Fax: 952-216-0135
E-mail: Solomon@smig.net

ISBN: 0615430120
ISBN-13: 9780615430126

Table of Contents

v   Acknowledgements

vii   Preface

Something Mom Used To Say, "Keep crying, and I'll give you something to cry about!"

1   The Debt Monster!

Mom taught me, "If you can't be honest with yourself, you can't be honest with anyone."

9   Credit: Your secret to the Good, Bad or Ugly.

Mom taught me to finish what I started, "Shut the door! Were you born in a barn?"

21   Legal Documents: Your Life Preserver.

Mom taught me about safety, "People don't drown by falling into the water, they drown by staying there."

31   Mortgage Madness

Mom was taught, "When you buy a house of your own, pay it off as quickly as you can."

39   Estate Taxes: Are You Exposed?

Mom taught me about forethought, "Make sure you wear clean underwear in case you're in an accident!"

49   **Life Insurance: The Best Kept Secret for a Tax Free Retirement**

Mom taught me the secret of life, "The secret to longevity is to keep breathing."

61   **The 401(k) and IRA Trap**

Mom taught me about options, "You don't need a paint brush, you need a wall covered in paint."

73   **The ROTH Dream**

Mom taught me about attitudes, "It's wrong to complain about things that I permit."

77   **The Annuity Attraction**

Mom taught me about timing, "If you walk away, then tomorrow will be no different than today!"

85   **Investment Properties**

Mom taught me how to investigate, "Would you just look at that dirt on the back of your neck?"

95   **Identity Theft: Keep Your Assets Along With Your Sanity**

Mom taught me about organization, "Get this room cleaned up, or so help me I'm gonna knock you into the middle of next week!"

103   **Closing Thoughts**

Mom taught me about wisdom, "Lending money to friends creates amnesia."

Acknowledgements

My lovely bride of 28 years, Michelle, along with my two children, Connor and Kelsey, deserve a special honor of thanks for putting up with me while I wrote this book. My many sudden audible sighs, imperceptible mumblings under my breath, and out of the blue statements I made while researching for this book, would be embarrassing had someone been recording me. Thanks guys.

I also want to tell you about Dr. Eric Shoars, author of 'Women Under Glass", and a personal friend. He was invaluable to me for some phrases I used, and clearer ways of communicating a thought or concept. He's a great word smith. Thanks man.

My clients also get thanks. Without them, I would have never been exposed to all these various circumstances I had to solve for them. I've grown over all these years because of them, and they have graciously told others about what I've done for them. Thanks to all of you.

Preface

Something Mom Used To Say, "Keep crying, and I'll give you something to cry about!"

Your mom said that too? Maybe there's a secret class they go to or something. I've taken a lot of classes myself. In fact, so many classes during my financial career of over 27 years, I see a trend taking place where it's becoming more and more common for people to do just that. They cry, they whine, they complain about everything. You know these people too. They are everywhere. Everything is everyone else's fault. No one takes responsibility for anything anymore, including their financial choices. I'm appalled by the lack of financial literacy I hear about in meetings, see on the television, hear on the radio, and read in the periodicals. It's an epidemic. The expectations we have set for ourselves, AND OUR CHILDREN about what we are capable of doing, or learning, or achieving, is so low, it's an insult and is an embarrassment to all of us. So finally, I decided to write a book.

Let me explain what this book is and isn't. Go to your local book store or library and you can spend all day just reading the titles of all the business books and the books about money. I've read my share of them. While some are great, others are great at getting it wrong and deceiving the masses.

This book is going to be as simple and as short as I can make it without stealing from you. By stealing I mean withholding critical information from you that you need to make an informed decision. The last thing I want to do is write a bunch of boring facts about a boring topic that will cause you to either put the book down and forget it, or be so exhaustive that it's over your head and you will forget the bulk of it anyway! Both of us lose.

My intent is to teach you through disclosure, what you need to know, but NOT make you an expert. Why? Unless you're going to be in the business, it would be boring, dry and complete overkill to give you all of it. Then you will get lost in the less important details and miss out on the concept I want you to learn. If you are, or will be, in the business, this book isn't going to be part of the curriculum you'll need for you to pass your classes and exams anyway, so what's the point?

Some things you will come across within these pages may shock you, make you mad because no one ever told you before, or cause you to sigh in relief because now you get it. I'll tell you right now that this message IS NOT traditional in nature. Those traditional guys are a dime a dozen and most of the people that listen to them, or that message, are struggling for their financial lives. I have purposely left out illustrations and graphs and numbers because they can be spun, misleading, and confusing. I don't want that for you. Confusion is one of your worst enemies.

I don't want you to watch me on Good Morning America some morning having to defend an illustration or graph that is unique to a would-be client for specific reasons, but taken out of context, as an approach for everyone. The good people at GMA would not do that, but don't miss the point. Other people in the business would not hesitate to try and make a name for themselves by trying to change the message to create doubt and confusion. I want to drill into you the more important concepts. Yes, we can go deep on concepts if we want to. They are the underlying principles and knowledge you need to help you identify more clearly what your choice should be.

If you attend my seminars or focus groups, you'll see me hold up a book written in 1777 called 'The New England Primer'. It's one of the 1st grade textbooks from that time. I used the word 'embarrassing' earlier, and I will use it again. It's a crying shame what our first graders in 1777 were expected to learn and achieve compared to our first graders today. For example, first graders at that time were expected to accurately spell and define 6 syllable words like, edification, mortification, familiarity and abomination. What are our first graders expected to learn today? Play nicely with others, share your toys, and 'See Spot Run.' I use this example to illustrate how the expectations we have for ourselves, in all areas of life, have fallen so dramatically. One specific area is how our financial literacy has fallen to shameful levels. It's almost as though our society is under some sort of spell that keeps us lazy, uncommitted, distracted, and lethargic. Everything but informed. For my part, I'm going to do what I can to change this paradigm.

I'm motivated to do this project because I grew up in a family of seven kids. I am the middle child and our family is no different than any other large family in the country. I saw and felt the struggles and challenges of having little money, and watching my parents try and figure out how the bills were going to get paid. I would make up excuses why I can't go out to eat or go on some simple event or party with the rest of my friends because we couldn't afford it. Listen, I know it's not the end of the world having to live on a meager or tight budget, HOWEVER, if there's something that can be done to improve your circumstances through knowing how money works, then why not do it? If I can peek behind the curtain and see the rest of the facts and information that wasn't expressed, then I believe it's worth it and it will affect the rest of my life. And by default, yours!

For instance, did you know that you can earn an average of 20% rate of return on your money, and lose 20% of your account balance AT THE SAME TIME! It's true guys. I'll show you how in the pages of this book. It happens everyday, and you need to know how to recognize an uninformed, or deceitful advisor that's giving you only half of the story. So thanks for buying the book. Let's begin!

The Debt Monster!

Mom taught me, "If you can't be honest with yourself, you can't be honest with anyone."

Mom used to ask me what's keeping me awake at night. I think I can finally, after all these years, accurately answer that question. It's what I've written about in this book. All these topics can keep a person up at night. Look at the table of contents. Have any of these topics ever kept you up? I thought so. Let's deal with them together. First up, 'Debt Reduction'.

This topic of debt may be the single most guilty culprit for keeping people up at night. As well as being responsible for ruined marriages, or at least strained relationships. It also destroys credit ratings, which in turn causes higher interest rates on loans like mortgages and cars. Bad credit hurts insurances as well. Debt just isn't anyone's friend. So how can we keep it manageable, or even non-existent?

Let's start on the same page by defining debt. Simply stated, debt is any financial obligation that has a time line associated with it. Credit cards, mortgages, car loans, school loans, cable TV, magazine subscriptions are just a few examples. However, the electric bill, fuel for your car, and natural gas for the furnace, are not considered debt. Those are expenses because they are ongoing in nature. You can ask the lender how much they need to pay off the car. You cannot ask the utility company how much to pay off the light bill. It's on going as long as you live there. Ok, we're straight on that.

As a tax and income specialist, I find people money by protecting them from losses they aren't even aware of at the present time or in the future. I meet with people in my office who can't afford to start addressing the future needs and demands of retirement and healthcare issues because they are buried in debt. That is the main area of concern for them right now. Is this you? Here's what I want you to do. Go grab a pencil (so you can erase if you need to) and a pad of paper. Really, go ahead. OK, now put a line right down the middle. On the left side at the top, write down MUST PAY, on the right side at the top, put down EVERYTHING ELSE. Good. Now, on the left margin of the left side the ONLY thing I want you to put there are the things you HAVE TO PAY to survive. No, cable is not a 'have to' item. Although, ESPN is a pretty good argument. No its not. Then on the right side, but still under MUST PAY, write down what the dollar amount is for that item. Example: Mortgage or rent. Light bill. All types of loans. Credit cards (minimum amount is all I want you to write down). The list on the left should be fairly short.

Now, under the EVERYTHING ELSE side, list, you guessed it, everything else. I mean everything!! With its corresponding costs. Take your time, this isn't a race. Think about everywhere you go and everything you buy. Here are some typical ones that are easy to forget about. DVD rentals, coffee from Starbucks, baby showers, birthday gifts, Christmas gifts, dues, memberships, sports team stuff, unnecessary clothes and shoes (impulse buying), buying lunch everyday instead of taking a lunch, buying brand food when the name means nothing once it's out of the package (most of the time anyway), quarterly payments on things, foolish single purpose trips in the car, maybe quit the soda and chips, plus so much more. Just think. It'll come to you.

Finally, add up the two sides separately. At the bottom in big numbers put down your income(s). Is it more or less than the total of the 2 sides combined? If it's more, good. If it's less, you can still be helped but it will be more painful and you may throw up your hands and say forget it. I hope you don't because the only one it will hurt is you.

Congratulations! Whether you know it or not, you just put together the beginning of a budget. If you are truly serious about reducing or eliminating debt, then you must take action with this list. Here's what you do now. Take to heart what is on the right side of the sheet. Will your life fall apart if you don't have some of those things in your life for awhile? Not forever, just until you get a handle on things. Here's a different way of asking the same question. **Will** your life fall apart **_unless_** you do something about these things? You need clarity and perspective about what's important and what isn't. This is where the rubber meets the road folks. Here is where you find out how mature you are as a person and how fiscally responsible you are with 'your stuff' and your money.

Your marching orders are this: Get rid of the fluff! Cancel the magazines. Cancel the cable bill. Get rid of the land line phone if all you use is your cell phone. Quit going out to eat. Stay home and cook. It's more fun than you think. You don't have the time right? Yea, I hear that all the time, but yet you have time to go to a deli and stay there for two hours chatting about how you have all these problems. I'm not buying it. I'm not asking you to go cold turkey. I know better than that. It will be too drastic and only frustrate you even more where you'll just end up doing nothing and be right back where you started.

Sometimes you have to do something you hate, to get something you love. If you don't address your debt and by default, your credit, by making some sacrifices, and being honest with yourself about what you spend, the long lasting impact could very well bankrupt you. It could keep you from getting a job, being turned down for loans, and much, much, more. If you have children, think about the message they are getting. I know that some of you are legitimately in a hard place right now due to no fault of your own. I get it. You lost a job that had nothing to do with your performance, it was cut backs. I feel really bad for all the people out of work, but don't lose your focus. It's even more important not to have a pity party. Take action now.

How do we get it paid off?

Go back to your pad of paper and start a new sheet. Look at the list from the MUST PAY side I had you create. I want you to copy everything from that list that is a **DEBT**, that has a timeline, over again, down the left margin in no particular order. No expenses allowed. Got it? Now, move to the right a little bit and jot down the balances of each one. Don't know what they all are? Find out! For now, though, put down your best guess. This is why you're using a pencil. Next, to the right of that, put down the MINIMUM payment the company wants you to pay. DO NOT put down what YOU pay! If you pay extra on one or two of your debts, I don't want to know about it right now. We'll get to that in a minute. In the next column, I want you to prioritize the debt based on the total balances of each one. If there are nine debts on your list, put a #1 for the debt that has the _smallest balance_. Find the next smallest balance and put #2 by it. Do it for all of them. Holy smokes, we're getting really close now. You almost have a bulletproof plan of not only paying off debt, but doing it the fastest, smartest way known to man. Here it is. Your list should look something like this.

DEBT	BALANCE	PAYMENT	PRIORITY
Mortgage	$98,663	$892	5
Car #1	$7789	$317	3
School Loan	$21880	$424	4
Credit Card 1	$6700	$134	2
Credit Card 2	$1475	$29	1

I want you to pay the minimum payment on every debt on the list EXCEPT #1. DO NOT argue with me that you should start with the debt that has the highest interest rate. That's why I didn't even have you record what they are. IT DOESN'T MATTER! Others have already tried this argument and failed. Focus on #1 and throw as much extra money as you can at that debt from the things you cut out on the 'Everything Else' list.

If you are curious, you can now divide the balance of that debt by your new higher payment and it will give you a close estimate of how many months it will be before that debt is paid off.

Typically, since it's the smallest debt, it is paid for within a couple months. Can you figure out why I'm having you start with the smallest debt first and ignore everything else? It's because you will make progress faster. So what? Hey, the quicker you shave off the debts, the more encouraged you will be. The faster your credit score will go up because debts are gone (it's a ratio thing) and the more motivated you will be to 'find' more money to throw at this fiscal cancer. Just trust me and do it. This will make a huge impact on reducing debt.

Now that you have an idea of what your 'discretionary income' is, use it and KEEP IT in your monthly budget. Wait, wait, wait. What is discretionary income? It's the extra income you freed up for yourself in the previous exercise. It's the total amount of money you took from other places, combined with any extra money you may have had before we even started this chapter, plus any extra money you were foolishly throwing at other debts out of order. Like your mortgage or car loan.

Ok, back to your debt. Let's say that you're throwing a $150 a month on a debt that only requires $22, like a credit card balance. When that debt is gone, you keep that $150 dollars in your budget and 'roll it up' to the #2 debt on your list. The $150 dollars PLUS the minimum payment of debt #2 will accelerate that payoff. A few more months and that one's gone. Take all of that budgeted amount and throw it at debt #3. You get the picture now? By the time you make it up to your #1 debt, normally your mortgage, you are really on a roll and making some serious headway because you're paying so much more toward paying off the debt.

Now the harassing phone calls have stopped, your stress level has dropped and you're enjoying life again. Now I'll let you go get ESPN if you want. **CAUTION: DON'T ABUSE YOUR NEW FOUND FREEDOM AND GET RIGHT BACK INTO**

DEBT AGAIN!! You just wasted my time and yours. Be fiscally responsible. Teach this simple system to your kids and grand-kids. The schools sure won't, I can promise you that. Good luck and welcome back to the good life. Now let's fix your credit.

Credit: Your secret to the Good, Bad or Ugly.

Mom taught me to finish what I started, "Shut the door! Were you born in a barn?"

In any house, shutting the door is always the last step when leaving or entering a room that led outdoors. It is also much more noticeable to people when there was a vast temperature difference between the two sides of that door. That change in temperature is what made them react so quickly and negatively to you.

Credit does the same thing. Wherever you go throughout your life, your credit goes with you. Good, bad or ugly. So when people pull it, they know right away if you leave 'doors open' or not. Those open doors are late payments on obligations you agreed to pay. It's debts that you decided not to pay at all. Can you feel the temperature dropping here?

Here is a short list of things that 'good' credit or 'bad' credit will affect: Home loans, business loans, vehicle loans, employment opportunities, renting, leasing, credit cards, rates on insurances, and even your ability to get some professional licenses.

If you're one of the millions of people with bad credit, I need you to understand something: Just because we are products of our past, doesn't mean we have to be prisoners of it! You can change. Not overnight, but it will come.

General Information and Common Myths About Credit

General Facts:

> Having good credit, and I'll tell you what good credit is in a moment, will generally net you 2 – 5% better loan rates. More cash flow for you.

> It will lower insurance costs. More cash flow for you.

> It will improve your chances of renting or buying the place you will live. Lower rates. More cash flow for you.

> It will also help you land that job you so desperately want. More cash flow for you.

Is it just me, or is there a pattern here? Cash flow is king. Speaking of cash flow, (how did you like that segue?) the credit card companies have been given permission by the feds to increase their minimum payments due on their cards, from 2% up to 5%. Who do you suppose will be the group they apply the 5% minimum too? You got it. The people with the worst scores.

Common Myths:

> Credit counseling improves your score. WRONG!! It slaughters it! You should be aware that the credit bureaus own the

credit counseling services. The bureaus AND the counseling service companies are privately owned companies. They are in business to make money. You should also know that these counseling services have *a whopping 90% failure rate*!! Now put on your thinking caps and focus. Is it in the best interest of the credit bureau to help you get a better score? None whatsoever. Why? Because it costs them money if you improve your score. The bureaus collect between 3 and 4 BILLION dollars per year in fees for credit checks. *Lower scores* mean more attempts (credit checks) to find a bureau that has an edge over another one. Every search a bank, a car dealership, an employer, ANYONE does, creates a fee for the credit bureau. More on the counseling service a little later.

> Paying off old accounts improves your score. Wrong again! You will go backwards at first, then, down the road, you start to improve. I'll give you more on this one later as well, under collections.

> You shouldn't use credit cards. Wrong, you NEED activity to create a history of being responsible. Remember, the lender is pegging you as a credit risk until YOU prove them wrong. No history means no proof of responsibility = a higher rate.

> Cancel your cards. If someone says you shouldn't have them at all, that's wrong. (See above. You need activity.) The last thing you want to do is cancel a card that has a good history tied to it. Never do that. Keep it, but use it responsibly. This decision hurts your overall ratio as well. They (the credit bureaus) look at the TOTAL amount of available credit extended to you and then they look at the total amount of credit you have used. If you cancel a good card with a good

history on it, you just narrowed the gap between your overall balance of credit available with the amount outstanding. The result is always a hit against your score. If you want to cancel a card because you have too many (over 4) and/or one carries a high interest rate, then that's a legitimate argument. In fact getting your number of cards down to 4 or even 3, will improve your score.

> Switching cards to get a better rate. This is dangerous. You will leave a trail when you use this technique and the companies will see it all guys. It will catch up with you and it will increase your rates.

Nationally, the average credit score is going down. This is mostly due to the economy and resulting job losses. No income, equals no payments on your "stuff'". *Simultaneously*, the creditors are increasing the standards for getting credit at all. So you have two parties, (you and the lender) going in opposite directions. It makes it tough for you.

What is considered good credit? A score of 720+ will get you the benefits I listed above. Here's a quick note for you. The higher you get your credit, the harder and faster you will fall if you blow it. *Just one 30 day late payment on a mortgage can drop your score 100 to 140 points*. Just like that. As teenagers would say, "Dude, you left the door open." People noticed.

You should also know that every time your credit is pulled, it affects your credit by about 10 points. So be picky about who you allow to do it. Since they are supposed to have your permission first, turn down the six requests to 'find out if you qualify' from the car lots you visited until you know which car you actually want. By the way, finding out if you qualify is just another way of saying, "Give me a minute while I go pull your credit."

How is your credit score determined?

Let's take a look. I spoke about having a good history earlier. As it turns out, this one topic accounts for **35%** of your credit score. Pay your bills on time people! It's the biggest factor in the calculation.

The amount of debt you have in relation to the amount you have available to you, makes up **30%** of your score. It's that ratio I was talking about.

Related to the history is the length of your history. Having good history is one part. Having a LONG good history is another part and equals another **15%** of your score. So we're up to 80%.

Another **10%** comes from the types of credit you are paying on. Credit card payments are a different type, or class, of credit than the mortgage, which is different still from a car or school loan.

The last **10%** is figured on any new credit you add to your picture. Don't read too much into this one. It's complicated how they come up with it and you could, or already have, misunderstood who that applies to.

Payment Strategy

The most obvious and the most important thing you can do for yourself is to always pay on time, if not a little ahead, in case there's a processing snafu (that means a mistake). Just shut the door each month. It's the history conversation we had. BUT, if you pay just one measly little dollar per month more, the system software credits you with a brownie button, figuratively speaking, and it helps your score climb. Any amount over the extra dollar doesn't help you at all from a score perspective, it does give you a better debt ratio/let's get this fiscal cancer out of our lives perspective.

Another strategy is to keep that ratio I already explained to you, below 20% of your total available credit limit. You will lose 1 point on your score for every 1% you are over the 20% balance.

Example: you have three cards and between them all, you have a limit of $20,000 of total credit available. What's 20% of $20,000? Well (10% is $2000, so 20% would be $4,000) If you have a balance between the three cards totaling $10,000, you lost 30 points on your score. ($10,000 is 50% of $20,000. What's 50% minus 20%. It's 30%. 1 point for each 1% over equals 30 points)

You know how certain people are always willing to give you free advice, but aren't really held accountable for what they say. Here's an example. "Pay off your credit card every month right away."

Little do they know that when you do that, the lender has no time to report it to the credit bureaus. You WANT them to report. It's what establishes your good track record and gets you those benefits at the beginning of this chapter. My advice, is to wait at least one month before you pay it off. It's not the end of the world if you pay a month or two of interest in exchange for that great rating. You will make it back, and then some, by getting cheaper loan rates anyway.

Here's another one. If you have a 'secured credit card' with some lender, get rid of it as soon as you can. Reason, it has "I'm a loser" written all over it. We know it's not true, but the lenders don't and that's what matters. These types of cards basically say to a potential new lender that you can't be trusted. You posses a card that has some sort of collateral linked to it because 'someone else' doesn't trust you. So they say, "If they don't trust you, we won't either." See what I mean?

Now when I say, "get rid of it", here's what I mean. You write a short letter to the company responsible for the card. You explain that you want the account closed immediately. You include the card in the envelope and mail it to them. You keep a dated, signed photocopy of the letter AND the card for yourself as well. The point is to make a paper trail, or proof, of your instructions to them.

Another payment strategy is to create payments. What I mean is, if you have 3 credit cards, have a balance on all three. HISTORY is what matters, not balances! A $15 dollar balance is no different than a $1500 dollar balance, so long as you don't violate that 20% ratio I explained. I don't care if all you ever have is a $30 balance that rolls each month. That's enough. Remember, don't pay it off in whole. Pay the balance from the previous month only. It works! You've got to do it.

Credit Counseling Services

Ok, here we go. Mom used to say, "If you can't say anything nice, don't say anything at all." I guess that's it for this chapter then. Oh, all right. I'll try and control myself and be nice about credit counseling.

In case you forgot, I already told you that these credit counseling companies have a 90% failure rate, remember? If that's not starting off on the wrong foot, I don't know what is. I also told you that these companies are privately owned, and the owners are the same people that own the credit bureaus. With that backdrop, let's go. Here's a hypothetical example,

Jeff lost his job unexpectedly. He and his wife are typical Americans. They have a modest mortgage of $178,000 and a small car loan of $5400. They have 2 credit cards with a total of $7200 on them. Before the loss of his job, they were current on everything. Now they are behind on several debts and some expenses as well. A friend that "knows everything", tells them about his sister's, wife's, brother's dog's previous owner that used a credit counseling service once and maybe they should try it. The source seems credible enough, so they get an appointment. The 'counselor', (I use that term loosely), assures them he will take care of it. "Shoot," he says, "I'll even stop the harassing phone calls you're starting to get. The fee for 'helping you out' will be $xxx.xx PER MONTH! In exchange, we'll make the payments on these bills for you. Just pay us, we'll pay them."

Trust me on this one. If you have high blood pressure, sit down, and take a pill. Find all the fragile items within the room and put them someplace safe, Okay?

What the "counselor" failed to disclose to our lovely couple is this: He has no intention whatsoever of calling ANY of the creditors to negotiate a deal or making a payment. Why? BECAUSE THREE MONTHS OF LATE PAYMENTS HAVE TO GO BY BEFORE THEY WILL REPRESENT YOU!! Meanwhile, the phone calls not only keep coming, now there are more of them. I know. It's criminal.

Get this. When, and if, they do finally negotiate, the puny 10% of the people this actually helps still end up paying on average 60 cents on the dollar. Some a little better, some worse. Most give up! How you doing? Blood pressure okay? Good, because we're not done yet.

Collection Companies

If you promise to stay calm, I'll give you the low-down on these shysters. Did you know that a collection agency has six years and six months to collect a debt from the last payment date you made!! Oh yea, it's true.

Naturally, they won't tell you that if you refuse, the debt will disappear from your credit report. Let's say that you want to do the right thing and take care of a past debt from 3 years ago. Since you have character, you innocently, write the check. Here's what happens;

If that check is written within six and a half years from the last payment, wait for it… ALL the interest, ALL the penalties and ALL the fees now apply all over again. The six and a half years starts all over again. Every previous outstanding payment, are ALL late.

The check you wrote, (because you wrote it before you bought my book and didn't know any better), gives the collection agency, access to your account for the rest of the balance. WITHOUT YOUR PERMISSION! Yes, it's legal! They can make a withdrawal from your account to pay off the remaining balance.

They may also try to scare you into garnishing your wages. If you're not self-employed, they can do it. If you ARE self employed, they cannot. Although they will try and make you think they can.

Finally, if you decide to make a payment after being sent to collections, pay attention to this, DO NOT write a check. Either wire the money, or use a cashier's check. You will avoid the problem I just described.

Challenging Your Credit

If you are challenging a purchase or an account that you had nothing to do with, never say to the lender, the bureau, or the credit card company, "You're wrong!" Now you made it a liability issue. The level of helpfulness you may have received, just took a one way trip to YOYO island. ('you're on your own' if you're wondering) What you should do is ask for proof that the account even existed. Here's how: **Never** ask for more than three pieces of proof because there's a law on the books that says if you ask for more than three, they can legally ignore you. The three pieces of information you're asking for must be 'verifiable'. If they can't, they **MUST** remove it. Ask for how the payment was made. Ask them to produce the envelope with a date stamp on it. Ask them for the credit card bill. Ask them for a receipt from the company, the store, or wherever it was that you supposedly made this purchase. They only keep these records for 24 months before they get archived, which is much more trouble for them to retrieve.

Ok, let's wrap up this chapter. Let's assume for a minute that you in fact did leave the door open. You've got a trail of open doors following you from everywhere. What can you do?

Start by changing your habits. Get your act together and pay stuff on time. Quit getting into debt in the first place, and stick to a budget. (see my DEBT chapter for more help on this) Then call the banks, the department stores, and credit card companies and see if they will work with you to take a smaller payment, give you a lower rate, and/or forgive some of the debt.

If you choose to use a 'Credit Repair' company that does what's called a 'rapid rescore', keep in mind that nothing's free. This technique works well. You can get meaningful improvement in five to seven days. These guys are not a counseling service described above. They are pros. They know the law and use it masterfully to force the bureaus and the credit card companies to play nice. However, it costs $50 per account, per bureau. That can add up in a big hurry. That's just the big three bureaus, Equifax, Trans Union and Experian. I bet you didn't know that there are over 100 credit bureaus did you?

See, you learned something. If this chapter was painful for you I understand. In preparing for this chapter, I took a special class to learn the secrets that aren't in any book or disclosed in any "public" class. It was painful to sit through. Our system is broken. I did you a favor by not disclosing everything I learned in this class. You don't need to be an expert on it; you just need what I told you. Remember folks, as long as you close the door, you'll be fine.

Legal Documents:
Your Life Preserver

Mom taught me about safety, "People don't drown by falling in the water, they drown by staying there!"

Hmm. There's some wisdom there. No one is immune from making mistakes, such as falling in the water. No one can control all outside circumstances that can have a negative impact on our life or the lives of our family. We CAN however take steps to enhance our financial safety against known and unknown laws and circumstances. Plenty of people experience a dramatic negative impact on their current and future financial well being by staying in the water. Let's see what documents you may want in your arsenal to get you out of the water and dried off.

<u>Short Form POA (power of attorney)</u> This document is used primarily for financial purposes only. Normally two pages in length, you will indicate on the form how much power you want someone else to have on your behalf. There is an alphabetical list, (A – N) of itemized, financially specific things you can individually permit someone to represent you on, or you can drop down to letter 'N' and check that one. 'N' encompasses the whole list.

You can also determine the length of time OR an event the form is good for. Example, you are closing on a home on the 3rd of May but you will be out of town. You can have the form for that day, that event and no more.

Additionally, some people choose to have no end date for the powers. Let's say you trust the person with your life. If something comes up, this person is your backup. Don't worry, you CAN change your mind! Just remember to file it with the city, hospital, doctor, lawyer and so on, so people know. Let any relatives know as well.

After you think it through, fill a POA form out, and complete the signature and witness blocks, make at least a half a dozen copies. In addition to the people listed above, you could do what my wife and I do which is to carry copies in the glove box of the cars. The emergency responders are trained to look there for registration, insurance and items like this. Now they know who to call and who has authority in case you're in a serious accident. *Put this document in your glove box along with the Health Care Directive below and you will be set in case the unexpected happens.*

One last thing, if you want something outside of the ordinary with this form, in other words you want to change it, you can customize the directive to do anything you want, but you will need an attorney at that point. Don't be foolish.

Health Care Directive This is a tougher document for many people to take care of because of the topical nature it deals with. That topic is being mentally and/or physically incapacitated. Others call this document by another name which is a 'Living

Will'. This document is a combination of the old 'Living Will' verbiage, only now it also includes the very important document called the 'Health Care Power of Attorney'. It's a two-for-one document.

Let's talk about the living will portion of it first. In it, you specify your wishes about how you want to be treated in the event you can't speak for yourself. If your doctor is speaking with your family and they are reading this document, you are in big trouble. You come right out and say whether you want someone to pull the plug. But under what conditions? Do they need 2-3 doctors in agreement about your dire situation or just one? Is there a period of time before that decision is even an option? Say 90 days. What about experimental treatment as a last resort? Do you want that? On and on it goes.

Then you need to disclose how you want to be handled in the event you don't make it. Is cremation what you want? Are you donating your body to science? Are you an organ donor before leaving your body for science? None of the above? Now you know why some folks avoid this document. Although it's not pleasant, it is a legal document that can save you and your family a lot of stress, risky guessing, miscommunication and potentially, lots of expenses.

Now let's look at the Health Care POA. You've done a good job up to this point. You took the time and energy to spell out what you want in the living will. Now the doctors and the courts are asking the next logical question. Who has the power to carry out what the patient (you) wants to have happen? Now is not the time to drop the ball.

Enter the health care POA. A cousin to the Short Form POA, this document deals with health care issues, not financial issues. You can name the same person for both forms if you wish but they are separate documents for a drastically different set of circumstances. Your health care directive instructs the doctors and the courts to abide by your wishes you have outlined giving so-and-so full authority to make health care related decisions on your behalf. Including, but not limited to, pulling the plug.

If you have told your family members and they understand your wishes if something happens, then when it does happen, the doctors and courts will have a hard time going against those wishes. By the way, the document can still be fought, but it's not only rare, it's an uphill climb. Unless you're a high profile person, your wishes will probably be carried out.

Personal Will There's a lot of confusion about what a Will does and doesn't do. However, I will just say that you should look into having one or updating it if it's several years old. When a person dies, other people want and need to know what to do with your "stuff". If you haven't answered that question for them, you force the courts to make that judgment for you. Some decisions may not go the way you intended had you been there to witness it for yourself.

As you know, a Will is where you specify who gets what. It sounds easy enough, but mistakes are made all the time. For instance, if you have an asset like a mutual fund account, there's no need to mention it in your Will because that account already has one or more beneficiaries named to it. Leave it alone, it will take care of itself. That goes for all your assets that have a beneficiary form connected to them. Just be sure your beneficiary form is what and who you wanted, otherwise, update it now!! Put down my book and make a note to check your beneficiary forms today or tomorrow at the latest.

The Will is where you want items like personal belongings, such as various collections (stamps, coins, dolls and so on), to get into the right hands. This is also where you would make your bequests. You know, those are the certain people or charities close to your heart that you want to leave money or specific items to. Beyond that, there's just not a whole lot more to do with this. Leave the stuff to your spouse and kids, say some nice things about everyone, and hopefully everyone meets up on the other side.

Beneficiary Forms Never, never underestimate the power of this form. Hear me very clearly. Are you paying attention? This form trumps your Will! If you have a life insurance policy for example, and the beneficiary happens to be an ex-wife, (because you forgot to update it), but in your will you name your current wife as the beneficiary, it won't matter. Your ex gets the money. Don't even waste time and money trying to fight it in court. YOU WILL LOSE!! The lawyer representing you doesn't lose, but you do. It doesn't matter what the asset is guys, it all works the same way. I recommend people do a beneficiary form check up about every three years.

Case in point. A client of mine in North Dakota, needed a Will and some other estate planning help. A lawyer was retained to write the documents. I drove to Fargo, ND to be in the meeting with my client and the lawyer to ensure accurate communication. One goal my client wanted, was to leave some money to five different charities from his 401(k) account and the balance to his wife. We discussed many other things and we left. A week or two later, my client sends me the Will and on the 4th page I read the list of the charities he wanted to leave money to. I'm glad he sent it to me because it would never happened. Those charities have to be listed on the 401(k) beneficiary form. Period! A good lawyer would have known that. I caught it and everything is going to be just fine now, but be careful with lawyers. Just because the "bar" gives them the right to draft a certain legal document, DOESN'T mean they should.

Things change. Marriages, deaths, divorces, along with age and financial changes, justify such attention. Just do it and know it is right for a few years at least.

TODD (transfer on death deed) This document is one of the coolest things since sliced bread! However, it's not available in every state. Currently this form is only available in 12 states and they are: Arizona, Arkansas, Colorado, Kansas, Minnesota, Missouri, Montana, Nevada, New Mexico, Ohio, Oklahoma and Wisconsin.

Why am I all excited about this form? BECAUSE, if you fill this form out and file it at your local registrar of deeds office, I just told you how to EXEMPT the total value of your home from probate when you pass away, that's why. If you live in one of these twelve states, I just saved you thousands of dollars! We're talking thousands people, **IF you will listen to me**. I just met with a family in Rochester, MN who will save just over **$65,000** because of this one form alone.

As of this writing, the National Association of Realtors puts the median home price in America at $265,000. If the average cost of probate is 4% of the assets listed in probate, I just saved the people in these 12 states on average, **$10,600**! You're welcome.

I don't know what it costs to file it in every state, but in mine it is $46 dollars. Nuff said. OK, maybe there's a little more to be said. There are different forms depending on your marital status. One version is for unmarried people. One version is for married people with BOTH names on the title. Still another version is for married people where only one or the other spouse owns it.

Lastly, in anticipation of your question, YES you can change your mind and revoke it. All you do is pick the form up at the same place you got the original one, or download it from your states website, fill it out and file it again. It's that simple.

Trusts I'm going to do you a favor. With the exception of the Revocable Living Trust, or RLT as it's called, I won't tell you about the other trust documents all over again right here. Just go to the chapter on Estate Tax and you will get all the information over there. Hey, I said I wanted to keep the book short. I'm true to my word.

The Revocable Living Trust (RLT), is the most commonly drafted trust. It is pretty straight forward and useful for most families. Why do people have them? Let's look.

➢ **Confidential.** These trusts are protected from probate which is a public forum. Having one keeps your stuff private.

➢ **Revocable.** It's in the name. You can change your mind, or revoke it. You can put stuff in and take stuff out as needed. What kind of stuff? Your home, your investments, your coin and stamp collections, bank accounts and anything else you want. It's called "funding" your trust. It's also the most forgotten and important thing to do. Your lawyer may have only drawn up the trust, but it's your responsibility to rename your property to the trust, otherwise, all you have is an expensive piece of paper. **NOTE:** If you decide to place your home in this OR any other trust, AND you still have a mortgage, pull out your mortgage papers and look for a transferability clause! It could read that if your home changes ownership (a trust counts), then THE ENTIRE MORTGAGE IS DUE!! Don't get burned here, it would be devastating. Lastly, you can decide to end it altogether if you want. Therefore, the flexibility of this trust is a real draw card.

➢ **Control.** More control than you may think. Not only can you call the shots from beyond the grave concerning your assets, but you can direct what assets get dispersed to what side of a family tree when you have blended family situations. Nowadays, blended families are common.

➢ **Safety.** Why are they safe? Mainly because you as the donor get to name who is charge of the trust after it's created. It can even be you! Your wife! Your fish! No not your fish. I was just making sure you didn't slip away on me.

Some people are under the impression that you only need a trust if you have a tax liability you are trying to eliminate or decrease in some way. This specific trust DOES NOT give you any tax advantages for creating it. The reason why it doesn't is because you can change your mind.

People do like the privacy of it and the control of the assets even after they're gone. Families that don't get along and are blended as well, make for a train wreck when it comes to deciding who gets what and why. Just avoid the whole mess by making those decisions before you go. That way there's no question and less stress and bickering among the heirs. (Hopefully!)

Now if you want to skip over to the Estate Tax chapter to read about the trusts and strategies that DO give you a tax break, you're excused.

Mortgage Madness

Mom was taught, "When you buy a house of your own, pay it off as quickly as you can!"

How many sets of parents and grandparents have said that over the years? Here's a small piece of wisdom for you. *We don't see things as they are, we see them as WE ARE.*

I fully understand why both my parents and grandparents said what they did. It's because of what they witnessed, and lived through in the late 1920's and early 1930's: The Great Depression. Back in those days, mortgages were 'callable'. It means that the bank can do just that. They call you up and say, "We're having a rough go of it, your entire mortgage is now due." or, "Since you missed your last payment, we are calling your entire mortgage according to the agreement you signed." Wait, it gets worse. Not only were residential mortgages callable, commercial mortgages were as well. So here's what's going on. Some Einstein, decided to invent and offer something called "Margins" in the investment world. It was a way of getting into the stock market for less money and controlling more stocks. Not only can you lose your entire investment, but actually owe more than your investment. People bought into it hook, line and sinker. Unfortunately, the sinker part is what they got.

The market crashed. Hard working men had the bulk, if not all, of their wealth linked to the market. Poof! Literally in a day, it's gone! Now they get a call from their friendly banker telling them to pay up or lose their home. I've read about and watched old footage from back then of people jumping to their death because they lost their wealth, their job, their home, and maybe even their business. That's sad and troubling.

This, my friends, is what our grandparents remember *and it still stings*. Their reasoning is this: When you have a home paid for, no one can come to your door asking for the keys. I'm not going to tell you in this chapter whether it's still right OR wrong to pay off your mortgage. It's a personal choice. What I'm going to do is educate you about the result of each decision and why some people are on the other side of the fence in this discussion. The other side says, never pay it off.

Here's some good news. Those callable mortgages have been outlawed since the 1940's. So don't stay up worrying that it can happen to you. It can't.

Should I Buy A Home Or Re-Finance?

It's a good question and a tough call. If I knew more about your specific circumstances, it would be an easier question to answer. Maybe the answer is neither. Here are some questions to consider first.

Buying:

    Why do you want to buy?

    Where will the down payment come from?

How long will you live there?

What is your monthly income and excess cash flow?

Is this a primary home, a second home or investment property?

Where is the home located? Is the area on the upswing?

What kind of mortgage do you want?

Re-Finance:

Will you be taking any or all the equity from your home?

Where will you put it where it will be safe from losses?

What kind of mortgage do you want?

Can you get a 'home equity line of credit' instead?

Will your cash flow support the new payment?

There are more questions, but they are more specific in nature so I won't bore you with those. Whether you want to buy a new home and you're an existing home owner, or you want to buy your first home, it is now much tougher to qualify. Even for those of you who want to re-finance your place. If your home is upside down right now, meaning you owe MORE than what it appraises for, the chances of updating to a new loan are slim to none. Also, the requirements have changed dramatically. Just a few short years ago the lenders had something called "stated income". It meant that you didn't have to prove your income. Now, however, the lender makes you prove everything! If you don't have provable, sustainable income and a positive cash flow, don't even waste your time. By the way, your credit better be above average to excellent as well. See the credit chapter for more about how to get above average credit.

Types of Mortgages

Let's say you find a lender and you actually pass the qualifications to buy what you want. Now you have a decision to make: What kind of mortgage should you apply for?

There is the old standby 30 year fixed mortgage. You could opt for the 15 year fixed mortgage. Some lenders are still offering an interest only mortgage as well. Anything else? Well, it's not tied to the bank, but what about a possible Contract For Deed?

Let's look them over. First I'll compare the 30 year fixed to the 15 year fixed. *Tell me why anyone would choose the 15 year option, based on the following information, over the 30 year option.*

The 30 year mortgage will generally be a lower payment than the 15 year mortgage resulting in better cash flow. The 30 year and the 15 year options are both fixed, so there are no surprises one way or the other. The argument I hear all the time is that you will pay your mortgage off in half the time, right? That is true BUT you should consider something else. If you have the cash flow to afford the payment of a 15 year mortgage, than you can still do it anyway, using a 30 year mortgage. Trust me, they will take your money. In essence, you haven't lost anything by choosing the longer 30 year mortgage.

Ah, but what have you gained? _Flexibility!_ If something totally unexpected comes up that affects your cash flow, like a job loss, you incur a medical expense or become disabled, your elderly parents move in with you, or any number of things. You are on the hook for less money per month using the 30 year option versus his 15 year cousin.

Should you choose the 30 year mortgage, AND you want to pay extra money on it, please listen to me. Write the checks separately! The first one is your ordinary monthly payment. The second one is the overage, in any amount, and you write in the memo line of the check, "Principle only". By doing so, you create a paper trail, and the lender isn't forced to try and guess what it is they're supposed to do with it.

Interest Only: This mortgage protects your 'Acquisition Indebtedness'. It's the term in the IRS code that is used to calculate your deductable mortgage interest. Let's say you finance a loan for $150,000. (this isn't what you bought the home for, it's what you financed or 'indebted' yourself for), an interest only loan never pays down that principle amount! Ever! You maintain your deduction and you have a lower payment. (most likely) These loans are available for different lengths of time. I've seen them ranging anywhere from 5 years to 30 years. What happens if your term runs out? You decide what you want to do. Get a different mortgage altogether or extend the current one, and so on. Now let's tackle the "Why" question, where someone would never pay their home off.

Should I Pay off My Home?

I must re-iterate here that there's no wrong answer. This is based on your level of education about money, mortgages, and the tax code vs. your comfort and stress level tolerance. So, you diehard 'never pay off your home' folks, don't judge the people who do. Likewise, you people that think it's dumb or irresponsible to keep a mortgage as high as you can, BE CAREFUL. They just may know something you don't. Learn from it. Here are some reasons people choose to never pay their homes off.

- *Deduction for tax purposes.* By keeping a mortgage on your home, you also keep your deduction for tax purposes. The type of mortgage will dictate how fast your deduction decreases, or if it decreases at all. (Like the Interest Only option we discussed.)

- *ZERO Return.* Your equity in the home makes a ZERO rate of return! Always, always, period! The equity is the difference of what you can sell your home for and what you may owe against it. That number, or amount of money, is buried inside the brick and mortar of your house. By pulling the equity out of your home every so often, WITH WISDOM, you are allowing yourself to capture a large, lump sum of money that can now be an employee for you. It's working for you making a rate of return.

- *Safety.* When the equity is removed from your home. The housing market can do whatever it's going to do, and you are insulated from it. If the market goes down, or depreciates in value, what do you care? You'll be overjoyed that you were on the ball and captured the equity before the market took it for itself. You already got your money out. If your home goes up in value, this is called 'appreciation' and it is NOT a rate of return on your equity. Then, *if it's appropriate*, take equity out again.

- *Tax Free Money.* The large lump sum you pull out of your home is a nontaxable event for you. It won't show up on your tax return as income. The IRS has disclosed it's definition of what income is, and taking a loan against your home is not on the list. What is? Wages, Investment Income and Passive Income, (like from a rental property). That's it. It's a short list.

- *Homestead Law.* If you have a high-priced home and leave a bunch of equity sitting there, you are a target for lawsuits. How? The homestead law (every state has the law, but differs on its application) only protects your home up to a certain level. In Minnesota, the homestead law caps out at $200,000. If you have a home worth $700,000 and it's paid for, some lawyer could sue you for the remaining equity of $500,000. If you can't pay, the court WILL force you to either sell the house or get a loan against it to pay the judgment. If you maintain a moderate to high mortgage on your place, then when the lawyer does an asset search to find out how deep your pockets are, it will be a deterrent seeing that high mortgage. Maybe to the point of saying it's not even worth it at all.

- *Rainy day fund.* Lastly, when you physically own or have the money in your possession, and you happen to lose your job or some other emergency arises, you now have the money to live on while you look for another job. You can still make your mortgage payments because you thought ahead. By the way, I have clients where this actually happened and it was a life saver for them! It got them over the hump and they never missed a payment.

IF it's wise to remove the equity from your home, NEVER, NEVER allow someone to tell you that it belongs in a security type product, like a mutual fund, a stock, or anything where the principle is not guaranteed and does not have a measure of liquidity to it. You're asking for trouble and people have lost their home because they needed their money and couldn't get to it, OR it wasn't there because the market took it.

Foreclosure

Let me speak to all of those among us who had the stressful and unpleasant experience of living through this process. Just because it happened to you, doesn't make you a failure. I'm dead serious about this, guys. Self worth and Net worth ARE NOT the same thing. Here are a few thoughts I go back to when I think I've failed. They help me re-focus. Maybe they'll help you too.

• Failure is not an event: it's a judgment about an event.

• Failure won't shape me: how I respond to failure shapes me.

• There's a difference between experiencing a failure, and being a failure.

Do any of these resonate with you? For me, they are all true and since life is hard sometimes, we need to renew our mind about what's true and what isn't. This chapter's done. Now, you can begin again with fresh knowledge, more experience and a better understanding of mortgages the next time it comes up. Here comes the "Estate" chapter. You ready?

Estate Taxes: Are You Exposed?

**Mom taught me about forethought;
"Make sure you wear clean underwear,
in case you're in an accident!"**

This statement also means be careful not to get caught off guard. For you, this means that if you don't take action with regards to your estate valuation now, it could have a huge affect on your heirs. It will cause a memory that isn't pleasant, and reflects poorly on you. Now is the time to increase your financial literacy! Finish reading this book. Then read some others as well. Might I suggest, Robert Kiyosaki's book 'Increasing Your Financial IQ" or "The Complete Book of Wills, Estates & Trusts" by Alexander Bove.

Exactly what is an estate tax anyway? You may have even heard or said things yourself like, "This law doesn't affect me." or "Only about 6½% of the people have to pay an estate tax." Those statements MIGHT be true, but as of January 1st of 2011, unless Congress and the President act, it most definitely won't be true for many more people. Don't you be someone that gets caught off guard.

The estate tax calculation includes the value of all your assets to determine IF you are susceptible to the tax and if so, to what degree. For purposes of the calculation, the list is quite extensive. Here are just some of them;

Homes, investment property, land, checking accounts, savings accounts, money market accounts, mutual funds, stocks, bonds, 401(k)'s, IRA's, ROTHs, stock plans, deferred comp plans, life insurance proceeds (if not in a life insurance trust), IOU's, unused vacation, unpaid bonuses, some trusts you are named in, installment loans owed to you, coin collection, stamp collection, antiques, tools, RV's, boats, anything of value. Get the picture now? The **I**ncome **R**emoval **S**ervice wants it all in the calculation.

In 2010, the estate tax calculation was this: No estate tax! At any level. In 2009, a person's estate balance had to exceed $3.5 million before a tax was levied. The rate was 45 cents on the dollar. As of January 1st 2011, the total estate balance will drop to only 1 million dollars and everything over that amount is levied at 55 cents on the dollar. (Even if the White house extends the Bush tax cuts, don't look for them to be delayed any longer than two years.) Do you see it? Did you catch what happened? This is a _Double Tax Increase_. The benchmark for WHEN the tax applies came down, while the TAX RATE simultaneously goes up. This does NOT account for the individual states that also have an estate tax that they charge! Here in Minnesota, they are kind enough to start from the first dollar and tack on an additional 10 – 42% rate on estates that have a $1 million dollar balance or more. Ouch. Now you know why I said don't get caught off guard.

To help you understand, here is a list of the taxes that apply on an estate over a million dollars beginning January 1st, 2011 if no action is taken:

Federal Estate Tax	=	55%?, 45%?
State Estate Tax	=	10-XX%? Depending on your state (maybe no tax)
Ordinary Income Tax	=	25% average on your IRA, 401(k) accounts

You add those up and you have 90% tax against qualified retirement plans, and/or 65% tax on your entire estate balance over the exclusion. What I just told you is the actual law that's on the books as of this writing. For the last year or so, the media, the columnists, the legislators, people in the financial business and lawyers have all said that Congress was going to extend the law and calculations used in 2009 OR maybe even abolish the tax altogether (like 2010). Well, they won't abolish it, but maybe they will extend it until the next administration comes in. Now it would be political suicide to back up the clock and tax the estates that have already passed in 2010. Besides, with the spending that's taken place over the last two presidential administrations, the government needs the revenue just to slow down the backward slide that our country is experiencing.

Here is something else to keep in mind about what happens when you inherit assets. It's called the 'Step-Up' in basis. The rule works like this.

Your dad buys a stock years ago for $1 per share. Your father dies in 2009 and the value of each of those shares are now at $10. The step-up rule allows you, the heir, to receive those shares based on the current market value of $10 per share and therefore no taxes are due on the gain. In 2010, you decide to sell those shares for $11 each. You will pay a capital gain tax on that $1 increase in value. (As long as you held them for one year. If not, the tax due would be ordinary income tax.)

Here comes the sticky part. In 2010, the law-makers, took away the step-up in basis benefit to help compensate for the removal of the estate tax. Now look at the example.

Dad buys the stock for a dollar and passes away. You get it all BUT its value to YOU begins at $1. When you sell the shares, the gain is calculated for everything over that $1 original purchase price. Add to that the fact that the capital gain tax is going up to 20% in 2011 and it will be quite a hit.

People aren't aware that the step-up in basis will probably be going away as well. Everyone is focusing on the estate tax and trying to get it permanently abolished. First, like I said above, I don't think the estate tax will be permanently abolished. The government can't afford it. Second, the government just included millions and millions more people into the tax code by removing the step-up benefit that they would have never collected a dime from because these same people would have been under the estate tax threshold. IF the government keeps the estate tax and sets it at 1 million dollars AND they remove the step-up in basis benefit at the same time, then these guys have essentially hit the lottery. Time will tell.

Ways To Lessen The Estate Tax Hit

For all the spouses out there, keep in mind that you all have the benefit, or luxury, of using the 100% marital exemption rule. **IF, it's wise!** I say 'IF' because that may not be the best, or wisest thing to do. Let me explain. As a couple you estimate your net worth at about 3 million dollars. If you choose to use this rule, you will receive the entire 3 million, tax free. The rub however is now, when you die, the entire amount is passed to your kids. So? Well, if the estate tax begins at 1 million dollars, as an example, then the remaining $2 million is subject to the tax. So, what's 55% of 2 million dollars? It is a whopping $1,100,000. What state do you live in? Oh, we have to add another 10% (maybe more) on top of that. What's 65% of 2 million dollars? Now it is a $1,300,000 tax. Your kids just lost a whole lot of money that could have been retained. This is the best case scenario, without taking action. How could it be even worse? As mentioned above, if any of the $3 million is also qualified money, (IRA's, SEP's, 401(k) etc) then the ordinary income tax is levied on all of it as well. It's a stand-alone tax. So figure the highest income tax rate on that money too. Now we're into the 90% tax rate on those funds. Isn't this nauseating? I'll say it again, "What you don't know, can definitely hurt you!"

Let's say our couple from above read my book and understands why it may not be in their best interest to use the marital exemption. What can they do? Let's look at several. Keep in mind I'm NOT an attorney and I am NOT rendering a legal opinion. I am about to educate you about how these choices work, not that you should have one. Are we clear? Good.

Credit Shelter Trust: This option allows the couple to divide the estate between them in order to take full advantage of the federal estate exemption at whatever level it may be at the time of death. Example; Both trusts are established, one for each spouse, and 2 million dollars worth of assets out of the $3 million are placed into the trusts, $1 million each. This strategy just saved the kids $1.1 million. How? They took advantage of the maximum federal estate exemption of 1 million dollars *per person,* instead of one, 1 million dollar exemption without the trusts.

They still have $1 million unaccounted for though, right? You're paying attention, good. It will still pass to the surviving spouse tax free. Even so, there are additional ways of protecting that as well. Since they could die together in a tragic shaving cream accident, or something, we better plan ahead for that as well.

Irrevocable Life Insurance Trust: This particular trust may be the most effective and useful trust you can act upon. The sole purpose of the trust is to protect the death benefit of an insurance policy against estate taxes.

When you read the chapter on life insurance, you will find out (among other things) that a death benefit from a life insurance policy passes to the heirs, income tax free. (There's a rare exception to this rule but it doesn't justify an explanation for the masses.) It does NOT pass estate tax free, which is the point of this trust. BE ADVISED, this is an irrevocable trust! You can't change your mind, nor can you have any "links" to the policy. It's called "incidents of ownership" and it will blow up on you if you have the power to change a beneficiary, take a loan, change the death benefit, name yourself as the trustee and more. The gifting law MAY also come into play here depending on the amount of the premium. The gifting explanation is below.

Overall, this trust gets an 'A' grade for reducing the estate tax and for replacing wealth that was given to a charity because of high appreciation, and still keeping the family happy by ensuring they get an inheritance.

Gifting: This is a great way to legally, quickly, and effectively transfer money out of your estate and escape the corresponding taxes of the asset. Here's how it works and why this option is one of my favorites for people to consider.

There are two gifting laws in play. The first one is an **annual gift exclusion** that has no limit as to how many people you could give money too. Currently, the level is $13,000 per year, per person! So, a husband AND a wife could each give a total of $26,000 between them to the same child per year. You have 4 children, no problem. The two of you could give, if you can afford it, $104,000 to the four kids in one year. NONE OF IT is taxable to either the parents, OR the kids! Yes, tax free. Nice.

NOTE: The gift must be "Present Interest" to qualify as a qualified gift!! Someone please ask me what "present interest" means. Anyone? Thank you. It means that the person receiving the gift must actually get it in the year you give it. Huh? If you think you're giving a gift by paying a $5,000 installment into an IRA where the person is the owner, you would be wrong! Why? Because the person getting the gift has restrictions to the money, therefore it doesn't qualify. You would need to give the person the $5,000 and they would have to put in the account. Or not!

What if you don't have kids? It doesn't matter. You can gift it to anyone you want. You could even give to me for that matter. No, seriously, you could. The law doesn't limit it to a relative.

The second way of gifting is the **lifetime gift exclusion**. This law allows you to give away to anyone, a total of 1 million dollars over your lifetime. Also, totally tax free. Give it all at once, or over a period of time. Even to different people. What ever you want. It removes it from your estate. You get to watch and enjoy the recipient use the gift, and most of the time it's going to the kids anyway right? Why not do it now rather than later. That is if you don't need it, of course.

The annual gifts that you make, in any amount **UNDER** the total cap per person, like the $13,000 for 2010, DOES NOT apply towards your lifetime gift exclusion!! In other words, the example I gave earlier where the couple gave away a total of $104,000 to their 4 kids will not lower each of their lifetime gift exclusions. There is still $2 million of gifting left on the table, $1 million each. SWEET!

How does your lifetime exclusion decrease then? In case you haven't figured it out yet, whenever you EXCEED your annual exclusion, the overage counts against your lifetime balance. So, if you give $100,000 to one person, in one year, then you will have a $13,000 annual exclusion AND an $87,000 deduction towards your $1 million balance. This leaves you with a $913,000 lifetime balance. Clear? Good. One more thing, whatever you use towards your lifetime $1 million exclusion comes right off the top of your Federal Estate Exemption amount. If you use $500,000 of your lifetime gifting benefit, you only have $500,000 left in your federal balance to use up at death. Why do it then?

BECAUSE, if you can afford it, you get the enjoyment of watching the recipients use your generous, heartfelt gift AND you just saved having to pay a lawyer thousands of dollars to set up expensive, complicated trusts to make sure you get that same $1 million benefit I just told you about.

Dynasty Trust: This option is less used these days and I'm not sure why. It is very powerful and effective for not only removing assets from an estate, but keeping it removed from your heirs' estates as well. Here's the skinny on this one. Find a GOOD ESTATE lawyer. That's first and foremost in getting this set up correctly.

By using a Dynasty Trust, the assets within the trust are not only removed from your estate calculation, but they are protected from creditors, and lawsuits, and, oh yea, if you're worried about naming a child as a beneficiary because you don't like the spouse, (hey, it happens people) not to worry. This trust also protects the assets from a lawsuit as a result of a divorce. Put another way, you can name your child, but the spouse is disinherited, period. How do you like them apples?

It doesn't stop there, though. As long as the asset remains in the trust, the beneficiaries will keep "beneficial use" of the asset(s). Meaning, they still get to enjoy "the stuff". As a parent or grandparent you decide to create this trust. You decide to name some expensive property to it, some healthy investment accounts, and so forth. If a beneficiary decides to take or remove an asset from the trust, then that asset **IS susceptible to lawsuits, creditors, and divorce proceedings.** So, beneficiaries, leave it in the trust!!

Another draw card to this trust is that the estate tax stays at bay for all the successive beneficiaries into, ready for this word, perpetuity. It means forever. Be advised that the length of time is different from one state to another. However, in all states, it's a stinking long time, okay? This trust protects the tree, not the fruit. This means the IRS can't tax the asset (the tree), they can only tax the income of the asset (the fruit).

Life Insurance: The best kept secret for a tax free retirement.

Mom taught me the secret to life, "The secret to longevity is to keep breathing."

At some point, breathing will come to an end for all of us. Then what? It depends on what you know and the precautions taken prior to death. Life Insurance: You May Not "NEED" It, But You Will Definitely "WANT" As Much As You Can Get! Did you know that a properly structured, cash value life insurance policy is the <u>BEST RETIREMENT PLAN</u> you can have? You don't believe me? Let me show you.

On October 3rd, 2010, the Wall Street Journal, one of the nation's foremost authorities on business and money matters, printed an article called, "Shift to wealthier clientele, puts insurers in a bind." It's a little long, but in a quick paraphrase, the article goes on to say the rich in this country "get it" when it comes to the benefits and tax advantages of cash value life insurance. In the mean time, the middle class is still scratching their head. The insurers are in a bind because the amount of insurance being written for the rich is so high. What exactly do the "rich" get that you're missing? I already told you. Life insurance is the BEST RETIREMENT PLAN you can have! It's also one of the most effective estate planning strategies out there. Now I'll tell you why. One word, TAXES! Or I should say, LACK OF TAXES!

The article uses information from the Federal Reserve dated 2007 and it says that the wealthiest 10% in this country own 55.1% of the cash value policies in this country. The wealthiest 50% own a whopping 93.5%. Put another way, half of the people in this country own 6.5% of the cash value policies in force. **Half of them don't get it.**

Listen to me. This is what the rich understand. The **right** plan with the **right** structure teamed up with a solid insurance company is like having a *ROTH IRA on steroids*, except the handcuffs of a ROTH, don't apply to this financial strategy. I said the RIGHT plan. Just because you have a cash value policy doesn't mean you're fine. Most likely you are far from it. Why? Because having the right structure, (the second part of my statement), is just as important.

Let's start from the beginning. You should be aware that life insurance in any form is the single largest tax benefit in the entire tax code. It applies to everyone, even if you are not a relative to the deceased. With a very miniscule exception having to do with business ownership, the entire death benefit of a life insurance policy passes 100% INCOME tax free to the beneficiary. The second largest benefit is the 100% spousal exemption. It's unlimited as well, but specific to a spouse only, which is why it's number two in the rankings. Now get ready to become smarter than everyone else on your block, (and many agents for that matter), about life insurance.

There are only two kinds of life insurance. *Term* and *Permanent*, that's it. On the surface, each of them contains five elements to them that I will list below;

TERM	PERMANENT
Low cost (initially)	Higher cost (initially)
Cost increases	Cost stays the same
Must be insurable to stay covered	Future health not important
No cash buildup	Cash that's liquid, tax free
Coverage ends (term is like renting a home)	Coverage continues (permanent is like buying a home)

There are many forms of each type, depending on the company (around 2000) you buy the policy from. Example; If you go with term, you can choose a 10, 15 or 20 year window of time that the coverage (policy) protects you for. Then at the end of that window, you will need to 're-purchase' the policy, only now at the older age which of course will be more expensive. You may also have to be *"re-insurable"*. Insurance companies love it when people buy term policies because a very, very low percentage of these policies are ever paid out. Think about it. When the new higher premium becomes a reality for you, most people DON'T continue to buy it anymore. It's too expensive. The company received all those premiums for all those years and never had to pay out a dime. If you choose permanent insurance, will it be a whole life, universal life or variable life policy? The decision you make right here, will have a lasting positive OR negative impact on you and your family for years to come! Why? Structure! Expense! Loan Provision! Crediting! Guarantees! Just to name a few.

There are only three kinds, (or categories), of money. They are: FREE money, TAX FREE money and TAXABLE money. Some of you are saying I missed one. Tax deferred. No I didn't. Don't allow your brain to trick you into thinking this money is separate. As we discussed before, any money called tax deferred (you should really use the term *tax postponed*) means you are still paying the tax in full, which is why it falls under the taxable category.

Free money. This includes gifts, (official or unofficial, determined by the size and if the tax code is used) grant money, and in some cases, inheritance. This type of money is the rarest and hardest to find. It's also redundant in its meaning, so I will not spend any more time on this type of money.

Taxable money. Examples include but are not limited to: Stocks, Mutual Funds, Corporate Bonds, Investment Property, IRA's, 401(k)'s, wages, tips, (yeah, right) Social Security, and lots more. To what degree and under what circumstances these financial instruments are taxed, differs one to the next, but taxable just the same. Some are taxed as ordinary income all the time, like wages and IRA distributions. Some are taxed at a lower capital gains rate OR ordinary income, depending on how long you held it. A mutual fund purchased in February 2009 and sold with a gain in January 2010 will be taxed as ordinary income. If that same mutual fund was sold for a gain in March 2010, it would be a capital gains tax because 12 months had come and gone since you purchased it.

Tax Free money. This category includes things like ROTH IRA's, Municipal bonds, and (you guessed it), Cash value life insurance. Now let's peek at these options real quick.

First the Municiple Bonds. If you have no experience or education with these, here's the skinny: They are safe. They are backed by the municipality that issued them. So as long as the city, county, school, hospital etc. doesn't go toes up, you're okay. BUT they just don't pay very well (low single digits) and they're not liquid.

Next, the ever popular ROTH IRA. I love these things, but they are not squeaky clean either. Since they deliver a tax free income, the government placed a deposit limit on them. In 2010, it is $5,000. The government knows how good a deal these are and if there was no deposit limit, why wouldn't everyone put all they can into one of these things right? That product actually exists by the way. I'll cover that in a minute. ROTHs also have the 59½ age rule and whenever you have that rule, its ugly twin sister known as the 10% penalty rule is also coming to dinner.

Another thing about ROTH's is most people choose to place the money in accounts that can lose value, like: you guessed it, mutual funds. Why? Because they spoke to some bank expert or investment person that doesn't have two nickels to rub together themselves but are somehow qualified in giving them investment advice and says that's where the money should be. So they blindly follow the blind and cut the check or release the funds from another account. What they really did is expose their account to a level of risk they may not understand or are prepared to handle. Not to mention more expense.

Don't get me wrong, these ROTH accounts are good to have, especially for the younger people just getting going in life. They don't have much to work with but want to do something. This choice is an excellent choice for them. Just be smart about where the money is held, that's all.

Finally, the cash value life insurance policy. In the ROTH discussion above I said the government had to place a deposit limit on a ROTH because if they didn't, everyone would get all the money they could find and place it in a ROTH. I also said that there's a product that actually WILL let you do that very thing. This is it. YOUR DREAM ROTH account. No deposit limits. No ugly twin sisters known as the 59½ age and 10% penalty rules. You have 100% tax free money coming back out. You have much more liquidity (no five year rule) and safety. Well, it's just easier to put it in a list for you what all the benefits are. So I did. Keep reading.

Now, if someone asked you which kind of money would you rather have, any reasonable person would answer: "Free money, then tax free money and last would be taxable money." With that answer as a backdrop, let's look at the reality of those choices. First, as mentioned above, the "free money" option isn't a realistic or viable option since it's very hard to get. If you have a way to get it, by all means do it! Grant money is free, but very specific on what you must use it for, like education as an example. Therefore, in real life, free money is off the table.

Next, let's look at *taxable money*. If options are available where you can diminish or eliminate the tax bite, why wouldn't you? When you look at the taxable options, don't forget that in most states around the country, ALL of those choices are also taxed at the state level as well. So while you are still breathing, you make your dollar. That dollar will be taxed at the federal income tax rate. For many people it will be taxed at the state level then at retirement (when you're mindful of every dollar), these income sources can cause another tax against your Social Security check. How do you like them apples? Now for nail in the coffin, (so as not to be repetitive), find out what the painful, last nail in the coffin is by reading the Estate Tax chapter, or the 401(K), IRA chapter. I can't bear to write again. It hurts too much.

Finally, the remaining option of <u>*tax free money*</u>. Remember the Wall Street Journal article and the people who "get it" with respect to cash value life insurance? The following information is one reason why people in the know, (many times it's the rich) have an advantage over the middle class. This is what they are buying! This is what you get when you buy cash value life insurance:

❖ Tax free accumulation
❖ Tax free cash distributions
❖ Tax free death benefit
❖ Tax free estate tax (if set up that way)
❖ Guarantee of principle in cash account against market loss
❖ Guaranteed minimum rate of return
❖ Competitive rates of return above minimum
❖ High contribution limits (no limit from law)
❖ Creditor protected (in most states)
❖ Access to cash
❖ Use for collateral
❖ Nursing home protection
❖ Disability protection
❖ Deductable premiums under certain circumstances

Look at the list again and ask yourself which benefit on this list is harmful to you? None. You're right. Now, compare these benefits against the things that you have right now. Out of 14 benefits listed, if you have something that reaps even five of these items, I'll be impressed. What did I not say? You're wondering about the costs right? You better be. I can't specifically answer that because the costs differ from one company to the next, one plan to the next, and one type to the next. Any new policy does have an advantage over policies that are three years old or older though. By law, any policy written after January 1st, 2009 must use the lower cost 2001 CSO table. This table is the maximum mortality cost per thousand of coverage that an insurance company can charge us. To help you understand the significance. There are only two other CSO tables out there. The 1980 CSO table, and the table from 1958. The number of policies in force that are still working off (charging expenses from) an old table are MASSIVE! You will be waiting the rest of your life for the phone to ring if you think the insurance company is going to inform you of the money you will save by upgrading your policy. Once you do find out what you can save and start the process of making a change to a different company and product, your existing company will bend over backwards trying to keep you and will even say, "Oh, we have that, stay with us." or "We can match that." Personally, I wouldn't fall for that line. They don't have your best interest at heart, otherwise you would have got a call about the rate drop. By upgrading, you can cut your expenses by over half if you're on the oldest table, and within sight of half if you're on the 1980 table. However, I will say this. I would counsel you, as I do others, to

NEVER BUY A VARIABLE LIFE POLICY. EVER!!

The reason... they are the most volatile AND the most expensive. (people in the business are screaming at me right now because they get paid so well for pushing these things). *Volatile*, because your extra cash is being placed into sub-accounts called mutual funds. So now, you _can_ lose money in them. From the above list you need to remove the guarantees I listed and the use for collateral because no bank is going to give you a loan against a contract that can lose value. *Expensive* because someone has to be hired to manage those mutual funds and those funds also have their fees intrinsic to the funds themselves. (Intrinsic means built in or part of) **Here's something I learned from my mom about logic, "Do it because I said so, that's why."** For goodness sakes, if there's ever a time to do what you're told, it's now! Don't buy these!

What should you buy then? My preference is *Indexed Universal Life*. These enjoy everything from the above list of benefits. They pay you a very decent tax free rate of return, with no market risk. They are not expensive, as a general rule. That's where having a good agent that has a clue and is looking out for your best interest is critical. From my chair, I would find a reputable independent agent. They have the freedom to shop the insurance companies and pick for themselves who they want to represent. It decreases the political stress of having to push a certain product from one company and the need to embellish the product or its benefits to make a sale. No sale, no food on the table.

Keep in mind that just because you find an indexed life policy with a reputable company, **it still** doesn't mean that you're in the clear. To make these policies really pop for you, the agent must design them correctly. Ask him or her if they are familiar with IRC 7702. USE THOSE WORDS!! If they give you the deer in the headlights stare, move on to another agent. Seriously! This is too important to screw up people. You want these policies to have the least amount of expense, which means the least amount of insurance coverage allowable by law. The above code refers to the MEC limit. It stands for Modified Endowment Contract and if it's violated, you lose the tax free status of the policy in regards to the cash value, not the death benefit. It's a corridor of maximum premium payments the owner of a policy can protect or 'deposit' inside it, and still be classified as an insurance policy.

"What am I trying to accomplish with IRC 7702 Shawn?" Great question! You want a policy that you can place the most amount of money into and have the least amount of expense coming out of it. That's what you want to accomplish.

IRC 7702 says that you can fully fund a policy in as little as five-seven years and never pay a single premium again. Here's a typical example: Steve and Jennifer are in their mid 50's. They have some funds in various accounts that are underperforming (that's a nice way of saying losing their butts) and are fed up with the unpredictable market. They talked with me because one of my clients told them how happy they were that during the huge setbacks in 2008, and 2001, they didn't lose a penny. *I'll say that again, they didn't lose a penny*! So, Steve and Jennifer decide to move $200,000 into an Indexed Life contract over five years. Steve now has a life policy that will never require another premium payment for the rest of his life. By the time they retire in 13 years, the cash value has grown on average 8.2% per year, tax free and is fully liquid to them. If they want any of it, there's no surrender charge to worry about and no interest on the money they take out. The large death benefit, should something happen to Steve, is 100% income tax free to Jennifer. The resulting return on investment received would be extrodinary. This couple is a real case! They will withdraw $72,000 per year for 30 straight years, TAX FREE! After 30 years, if he's still blessing us with his presence, there's still money left in his account to use if he needs it.

Here's something else I learned from my mom, "Don't exaggerate."

What I just disclosed to you may seem 'Too good to be true'. Believe me, I've heard this cop out a million times. I'm telling you, it's not too good to be true and I didn't exaggerate one bit. I know that everything I just wrote is verifiable in the tax code and with the insurance companies. Now the ball's in your court. What you do with this information will either discredit or substantiate the article in the Wall Street Journal. Are you going to do what the wealthy do? It's not rocket science. It has to do with financial literacy and taking action on what you've learned. Will you be above the 50% line or below it? Will you be enjoying the long list of benefits available to anyone 'in the know', or will you be the one whining and complaining about how the rich get all the breaks. It's up to you!

The 401(k) and IRA Trap

Mom taught me about options, "You don't need a paint brush, you need a wall covered in paint."

She's right! I didn't have to have a brush to get the job done. A roller would work. A decorative sponge would also work. Maybe the best option would be a pressurized paint sprayer.

Ever since the early 1970's the government has been telling the public that you need a brush, (401(k), IRA) to get the job of retirement done. They (the government) won't teach you how to use the brush though, or what size brush you need, nor will they tell you that you may not even need a brush at all to get the job done. They (the government) are your "friends" so just trust them because this is good for you and they have your best interest in mind. Sure they do. What's that you ask? How much do they (the government) make if you do this? Oh, don't concern yourself with that. They'll tell you later when you want your money back!

Just as many things are in life, there's more to these accounts than what meets the eye. The government gave us a sales pitch about these things that wasn't completely on the up and up. How? Let's say that they come to you with a check for $10,000 and they say "Go ahead, you need the money, cash it." What are the two questions you want to know? First, what's the interest rate you're going to charge me? And next, when do you want the money back? Their (the government) answer to these valid questions is this: "We don't know what we're going to charge you because we don't know how much we will need by then. But don't worry about that, just cash the check!" Would you cash it? I hope not, but people are doing it with excitement, everyday.

IRA and 401(k) accounts were created and presented to the public as doing us a favor. They said, "Let's let the public take control over their own investment choices and we'll stay out of it". First, the public wasn't prepared or educated enough to handle the responsibility of making their own investment choices, and second, the government didn't stay out of it. They have their bony little fingers taking your money away all through these accounts.

As a former broker myself for 16 years, I was taught by a system that was very purposeful about what I should say and what to leave out so as to make a sale. Whether I was speaking to an employer, a human resources person or an individual in the plan, the focus was to make sure the benefits were made very clear, and diminish the drawbacks. However, if you "forget" to mention one or two drawbacks once in a while, well, you're only human right? One problem I see is this: Who gets to define what a benefit is? Another problem is lack of FULL DISCLOSURE on those drawbacks. I now speak and teach people about some of these 'benefits' or characteristics as flaws and even reasons why maybe these type of accounts are actually harmful to many people.

As we unpack this retirement strategy, you will begin to understand what I mean, and if I do my job well, you may even be making funny sounds or muttering under your breath the next time some "expert" on one of the morning news shows, or an expert shows up at your company, rambling on about funding one of these accounts to the fullest extent. Ok ready? Let's break it down. To illustrate the restrictive, punishing conditions of these accounts, I'll refer to them as handcuffs.

HANDCUFF #1   TAXATION

Spoken of as a benefit, the IRA and 401(k) accounts are sold or promoted by brokers, employers, HR personnel, and even CPAs as a tax savings. Is that really true? **Absolutely not!** These accounts and others like them, all called "Qualified Plans", meaning if you follow certain guidelines they "qualify" for some break, are NOT saving the participant any tax whatsoever. Taxes are deferred or postponed until you reach a certain age or you decide to take some money out. When you do decide to remove some income, it is also important to understand your money could be taxed a second time. I'll deal with that one on the next handcuff. Now put down the doughnut for a minute and pay attention.

When you want to take, (or must take) your money back, you'll have to start taking it out at 70½, you are taxed at the ordinary income tax rates _at that time_!! Do you know what the rate will be? Neither do I. Neither does the expert you're seeing. Don't miss this!! I've done hundreds and hundreds of seminars over the 27 years I've been in the financial services arena, and for the last four to five years, I've been asking people which direction the tax rates are headed. The overwhelming answer is always up.

I believe them to be right. So that means that *if* your account balance goes up, you will be paying a higher amount to the government. Settle down, I hear you loud and clear. You bought the lie and so you argue that you'll be in a lower tax bracket when you retire, right? **Wait!** A few things come to mind with this line of thinking, so do yourself a favor and give me a minute.

First, if a broker or financial planner told you this, why on earth would you want to work with him/her? In effect, they just said "If you work with me, I'll make sure you're no wealthier later than you are now." Or "I'll make sure you're not making any more than you are now." Translation, you are poor. That's not why any of us wants to work with someone. They're supposed to know more than you and get you a rate of return that will outpace taxes and inflation. Inflation being the "hidden tax" people always forget.

Second, most folks have no children at home anymore and they have their home paid for so there are no real deductions to make use of to put you in a lower bracket.

Third, income taxes can go up in two ways at the same time! The bracket itself can be lowered so that you reach that bracket quicker. For instance in 2010, the 25% tax bracket for a married couple filing jointly starts at $68,000. Congress could choose to start that bracket at $55,000 instead. Therefore, you will be paying a higher tax sooner. The other way is to raise the rate inside that bracket. Instead of a 28% rate, they make it a 33% rate. Don't think this doesn't happen, people. In 1941, the *tax rate* was 81% but you had to make *$5 million* dollars (the bracket) before it affected you. In 1942, the rate jumped to 88% and it started at $200,000 instead of $5 million. A huge difference!

In case you were sleeping, this phenomena could happen again on January 1st 2011. If not, then in the near future. Read the estate tax chapter for more on this.

Fourth, the bracket you **postponed** your tax in, is **lower** than the bracket you take it out in. Example: you take a job at 22 years old and start your 401(k) account like all the other sheep. (Yea, I know, I've got issues) Your tax bracket is 15% because you're just starting out. You're in that bracket for 15 years. As you gain more skill and promotions, you jump to the 25% bracket, but by now you have some other investments doing well also. You reach 65 and throw in the towel. Your deductions are gone. You have IRA and 401(k) accounts on top of some other investments and your Social Security income. Your accountant says you have an adjusted gross income of $73,000. DO YOU SEE THE PROBLEM? You elected to postpone a tax that would have been out of your life forever in one of the lowest tax brackets available to you, in exchange for paying a tax in a higher tax bracket when you get the money back out. How much sense does that make? You lose! Big time!

Finally, had you been in the same investments OUTSIDE of the plan or IRA, the growth would have only been taxed at capital gains tax rates instead of ordinary income rates. Now for the cherry on top. Any losses you suffer in one of these accounts are all on you! No deduction is given to offset income. The same losses outside the account would have given you a deduction. The loss still stings, but it stings less when you can deduct it.

HANDCUFF #2   ACCESS

Your friendly IRS, or as I sometimes say, Income Removal Service, has thought ahead to try and make sure we leave our money in these accounts as long as possible. Why? They make more money. So, that's why Part 1 of the age discrimination law is in play with these accounts. Prior to 59½ there will be a 10% penalty for taking money from these accounts. The penalty is over and above whatever your tax bracket is. If you're in a 25% tax bracket, then add the 10% penalty to that. Below are the "exceptions" to the rule;

10% Penalty Exceptions as of 2010		
	401(k)	**IRA**
Death	X	X
Disability	X	X
72 T Distributions	X	X
Medical Expenses	X	X
IRS Levy	X	X
Active Reserve	X	X
Higher Education		X
1st Home Buyer		X
Health Ins (no job)		X
Age 55	X	
Age 50 public servant	X	
457 Plans	X	
QDRO	X	

If it happens to be a 401(k) you're taking money from, there is also a mandatory 20% withholding on your withdrawal. So if you need $10,000, you actually get $8,000 and if you are under 59½ another 10% will be charged against the original $10,000 amount. By the way guys, that 20% withholding doesn't go away, even if you leave the company. The only way to free yourself from the rule is to convert it to an IRA after you leave the employment of your company. And no, there is no tax due on the conversion. The other point I alluded to in Handcuff #1 is that the income you remove from these plans, can be taxed again by way of your Social Security check. The Social Security Administration has two benchmark income levels whereby if you exceed them, a portion of the income you receive from your Social Security check will be taxed at your current tax bracket as well. In essence, the same dollar is taxed twice! What does that look like? Under current law, here it is;

Income Level	SS Taxed
$32,000 - $44,000	50% of check
$44,000 +	85% of check

This is based on the married filing jointly table. You may be asking "What's income?" It includes withdrawals from these plans, wages, interest and dividends from investments, pensions, and oh yeah the Social Security check itself. Well, isn't that special?

HANDCUFF #3   DISTRIBUTION

Part 2 of the age discrimination law proves that the government boys aren't going to wait around forever to get their cut. Once you reach the age of 70½, you are *required* to take money out according to a predetermined multiplier in the tax code. The distribution will be fully taxed, as you know, but if you don't take enough, now you get dinged another 50% on the amount you didn't take. Fair? No. Law? Yes.

HANDCUFF #4 DEATH

IRAs and 401(k)'s may be the worst place ever to have money located if you happen to die. Here's my reason why: Not only is the account balance still fully taxed like it would be anyway but, depending on the size of your estate, it is taxed again. The estate tax starts from the beginning balance of your 401(k) and IRA accounts all over again and not the remaining balance of these investments after the income tax calculation has been applied. Oh wait, I'm not done. If you don't have a competent professional to help with the deceased's estate, you're staring at yet another expense by way of an overcharge on the estate tax calculation. Many if not most of the states have their own estate tax calculation as well.

Did I mention the extra tax against the same dollar coming out of these accounts against your Social Security check? Yea, I know I did, just don't forget. It applies while you're living and taking Social Security.

It is not unusual for the 401(k) or IRA account to be taxed in the 80-95% neighborhood when all is said and done. If people knew this taxing system was waiting for them on the exit strategy, I wonder how many of these accounts would actually be sold? Remember my example of the government giving you a check and they'll tell you the interest later? Here you go. The interest is the taxes that will be levied against you when you are taking your money back out. How do you feel? You need a break? A fan? Medication perhaps?

As if I haven't presented enough evidence as to why I have issues with these accounts, I'm not quite done yet. Upon death, if there's no spouse, the beneficiaries are forced to make a decision. They can either take a lump sum distribution, or spread it out over five years. Based on the size of the account, the first option can be absolutely devastating and the second option can be just plain bad.

The lump sum distribution pushes the beneficiary into a higher tax bracket, and therefore the corresponding tax rate leaves less money to the heir. Since this money is "income" it is added to the income the heir already made in that year. In most cases, it doesn't take a very large 401(k) or IRA account to push them into the higher or even highest bracket at the time.

The five year distribution cuts the tax hit into smaller bites, but it can still be painful if the account has much size to it. My suggestion is behind door number three. Find a professional in the business and have him/her educate you on the "stretch" option available to the beneficiaries. Most likely, the company that holds the deceased's 401(k) or IRA will not tell you about this option. *The "Stretch" distribution* allows the beneficiary to extend the distributions of the deceased's account over their lifetime. This gives the beneficiary much more control of the account and flexibility with investment choices, withdrawals and the like. Don't forget that no matter what the age is of the beneficiary when the account is inherited, the new owner **MUST** take the first Required Minimum Distribution or (RMD), by the end of the year **FOLLOWING** the year of death.

Example: Dad passes away on January 22nd of 2010. Mom passed away a few years before and dad never remarried. The 32 year old child must take an RMD before December 31st of 2011 on that account AND BEFORE the money is transferred to their own "PROPERLY TITLED IRA".

The 20% Lie

If you read the preface, you may remember my statement about how you can make an average 20% rate of return and LOSE 20% of your money at the same time. Here's how it works.

A broker, a financial planner and even the reps from the mutual fund companies themselves will sit across from you and try to sell you a mutual fund or some sort of investment that averaged a rate of return over the last two years, five years, whatever it might be. They don't tell you what the account is worth and here's why.

Let's say you buy a mutual fund and put $100 in it. Let's assume that you hit a home run where the account doubled in one year, therefore earning a 100% rate of return. You now have $200 right? The next year the bubble bursts and the account goes backwards –60%.

Mathematically, you are still up 40% (100 – 60 = 40) and it's been 2 years, so 40% divided by 2 years gives you an average rate of return of 20% per year. You with me? Ok, that's the math, NOW let's look at the money.

Year one you made 100% on your balance for a total of $200 dollars. Year two you lost 60%. What is 60% of $200? It's $120. Your account now only has $80 in it. You started with $100 and now you have $80 which is a 20% loss on your money, but your sales rep shows you 20% average return on their wonderful mutual fund. Get it? He told you the truth, just not ALL the truth!

I could go on but I think you get the point. I do have issues with these accounts and I really have a low tolerance for the so called 'experts' in the banks, the investment firms, the radio and TV shows that give the public just enough information to entice them to fund these accounts, to the fullest extent of the law if possible, and yet FAIL miserably in giving full disclosure about what happens when you want your money back! So be careful people! Next up: The ROTH Dream.

The ROTH Dream

Mom taught me, "It's wrong to complain about things I permit!"

If I had a dollar for every time someone was in my office complaining about a situation they put themselves into, or they permitted, I would be very well off today. Things like finding out too late the kind of person they really married. Starting out as a social drinker, but ending up an alcoholic. Letting the children dictate how the family is run, instead of the parents. On and on. I'm not making this up. Our moms all said this one, right? "If Bob jumped off a cliff, would you jump too?" Yet as adults, we do just that. Maybe the most common one I hear though is how mad they are that they invested in an IRA or 401(k) accounts, only to FEEL the pain of getting back out of them.

Despite the warnings, despite the written material explaining it, despite the seminars they attended, they chose to follow the masses anyway. Traditional thinking isn't always the best. They found out the hard way. Maybe you will too. Just don't complain since it's your choice to stay in a 401(k) or IRA and keep feeding the "beast", by contributing to it. I'm going to tell you about an option you can invest in, and never have to complain years later in someone else's office about your decision. I want you to know the benefits of, (AND the conditions of), a ROTH IRA.

So many people would choose to turn the clock back if given the chance so they could have funded a ROTH IRA rather than a Traditional IRA.

Quick Facts

If you want to know what the big hubbub is about, here it is.

	ROTH	Traditional
Tax free accumulation	Yes	Yes
$5,000 deposit per year	Yes	Yes
$1,000 catch up	Yes	Yes
10% early withdrawal penalty	Yes	Yes
59 ½ age restriction	Yes	Yes
100% taxable on withdrawal	NO	Yes
70 ½ mandatory withdrawal	NO	Yes
Tax deduction on deposits	NO	Yes
Social Security check taxed	NO	Yes
5 year rule	Yes	NO

Do you see it? The line that says it is 100% tax free coming back out? This is a big deal! People that choose this strategy pay the tax up front (which you do anyway) instead of on the back end. The wisdom here is that you already know what your tax rate is. It is behind you forever. You only pay tax on the normal income you have for the year, whether or not you fund a ROTH. You just don't get a deduction. You know what, I'll take that trade off all day long and twice on Sunday.

Some of you are wondering what that five year rule is. That's good because you should want to know. It means that from the time you open a ROTH account (it only applies to the first

ROTH, not subsequent ROTH's) you cannot gain access to the growth for five years OR, don't miss this, age 59½, whichever is FARTHER away!

If you are 44 years old and open a ROTH, then you have to wait until 59½ to access the gains. If you are 57 when you start a ROTH, you have to wait five years, or age 62, because five years was farther away than age 59½ was.

When does the clock start for the five years? Wow, I never get asked that. Thanks. It starts on January 1st of the year you opened the account. If you opened it on October 17th, 2006 for instance, the clock started on January 1st, 2006. Here is another cool thing. If you have four different ROTH accounts, this five year rule only applies to the oldest account. Each account after that points to the date of the first account. When five years have gone by, the rule is gone across the board. Cool!

If you love the benefits of this account, (and who wouldn't), but hate the $5,000 deposit limit, then you'll want to read extra carefully, my ROTH on steroids chapter. Don't see it in the table of contents? That's because it's in the life insurance chapter.

ROTH Conversions

The popularity of IRA and 401(k) conversions to a ROTH IRA is on the rise. For good reason. Taxes are on sale right now. Those who can afford it are doing themselves a huge financial favor by getting the tax out of the way before the tax rates rise. They will rise. You know that, right? So what happens when you choose to do a conversion? First, no one is forcing you to do it at all, or in any specific amount. If you want to convert all, a portion, or none of your IRA balance, it is up to you. Just know that when and if you do, that amount will be taxed on that current year's income, over and above whatever you make in other ways.

Maybe for you it's wise to only convert whatever you have left in your current tax bracket. Huh? If your taxable household income is $75,000 in 2010 for instance, you can convert $62,300 from an IRA or old 401(k) before you pop up to the next tax bracket. I just described the 25% tax bracket for 2010. Where will the 25% of $62,300 come from? That would be, $15,575. You better account for it somewhere.

WARNING: Do Not Convert If You Have Company Stock In Your 401(k)!! This could cost you. Do you like overpaying on stuff? That's what you'll do if you convert and don't call or write me. Remember my mom's statement, "Don't complain about things you permit!"

If you choose to fund an IRA or 401(k) account, thinking that postponing tax to a future date when the tax rates will be higher, as well as your income, hey, you chose to do it. Don't complain! If you convert a 401(k) to a ROTH without knowing the rule that can save you taxes if you have appreciated stock in there, then you brought it on yourself! Don't you dare complain about the extra tax you will pay! Unlike other mistakes you make involving ignorance of the tax code, this particular problem is one the IRS will not bend on. When it's done, it's done! I can turn the clock back up to three years on other issues, even after you pass away, and fix over payments on taxes for the benefit of your heirs, but not this one. ROTHs are great. There's no doubt about it.

The Annuity Attraction!

Mom taught me about timing, "If you walk away, then tomorrow will be no different than today."

As a child and even as a young teenager in high school, I struggled with some relationships. Big surprise, right? Yeah, I know. What teenager doesn't have this hurdle at some point in those years? But, I was also an easy target for bullies because I was too nice to insult people, pick on people, or fight back verbally or physically when I was being attacked. Guys, gals, take it from me, you do this for very long and it gets old.

Mom was simply telling me to stand up for myself. Don't be a doormat by letting people say or do whatever they want at my expense, with no accountability or consequences. Until I prove that I can and will defend myself then tomorrow will be the same as today. What I had going for me then, and still to this day, is the fact that I'm an athlete. It didn't matter what the sport was, God blessed me with a natural ability to pick sports up quickly and be good at it. I don't say this out of pride it's just how it was. So, I earned the respect from the popular kids and fellow jocks in the school. It didn't take long where other people came to my defense, because let's face it four or five on one just isn't a fair fight. I needed help and thankfully, it came.

Now it's my turn. I'm telling you boldly and directly, if you walk away from the guidance and wisdom in this book, then the challenges and problems you have now, will still be there tomorrow. All the chapters in this book won't apply to you, but I'm guessing many of them will. (Like the topic of this chapter as an example.)

The Big Attraction

Attraction #1: This investment has made a huge surge in the last few years because people are discovering that it is always *better to make nothing, than to LOSE something*! Translation, **SOME** annuities protect you from losses and still give you gains.

Attraction #2: Any one can have one. There are no medical requirements (like life insurance), no income standards, (like an IRA) and no gender, race or religious issues to mess around with.

Attraction #3: These investments are for the most part very flexible. You can deposit a lump sum. It doesn't matter where it comes from. It could be a different investment that's kicking your butt in losses. It could be equity from a home you sold. It could be an inheritance. It could be other things as well and a combination of them all. You can also deposit money monthly, quarterly or annually on top of, or instead of a lump sum.

Attraction #4: At some point in the future, you can opt to have income from your account for the rest of your life, AND you can tell the company that if you die within a certain period of time, you want those payments to continue anyway to someone else for a set time frame, (say 15 years), in case you don't live that long.

Those are some pretty solid reasons why they are popular. I do like them, <u>BUT, one reason why I DON'T like them</u> as my number one choice is my old enemy: Taxes!! Just so you know, the growth of an annuity is taxable. When you ask for money from your annuity, the law referred to as LIFO comes into play. It stands for Last In, First Out. Meaning, the last dollar in, which is growth, NOT your deposit, is the first money you get back, which is taxable.

Flavors of Annuities

Like many other investment choices, you hurt yourself by lumping all annuities together. They are definitely NOT the same.

Fixed Annuities: They are very safe, which is great, but since they are so safe, they also don't pay a very good rate of return. They do pay better than a CD and run of the mill money market accounts though. Therefore, they are an alternative to higher risk investment choices. They are simple, straightforward, and easy to manage since the money is not in the market.

Variable Annuities: I don't normally recommend these because you can lose your principle. These have sub-accounts of mutual funds which as most of you know, are volatile. Even though you can choose from THEIR list of funds, which ones you want, at the end of the day they are still mutual funds. These pay your sales rep very well, which is why they push these so much.

They are also the most expensive because they have to pay someone to manage the mutual funds PLUS, the funds themselves have their own fees and expenses built into them. Unscrupulous sales reps will tell you a half truth by saying that the principle is guaranteed, or even a minimum rate of return is guaranteed, however, they "forget" to tell you that you'll never see it, only the beneficiary sees it. Some variable annuities MAY let you benefit from a guarantee BUT you have to keep it for at least 10 years first, some longer, and then you have to select a certain restrictive payout option before they will actually make good on their promise. Very tricky. They made the disclosure, they just didn't say WHO OR WHEN it applies. Ask questions like these:

> Does that guarantee apply when I start taking money eight years from now?
>
> Does that guarantee only apply at death for my beneficiary?
>
> Under what specific conditions does that apply?
>
> Can you show me in the contract where it says that?

See what they say. See if they squirm because you're not supposed to ask that.

Indexed Annuities: These annuities are a hybrid of the first two above. You get your cake and eat it too. These are my favorite for the following reasons. They are as safe as the fixed annuity. They have a better rate of return than the fixed annuity offers. They offer a Lock-In and Reset feature which means every gain you receive, you always keep. These accounts can only go in one direction, UP.

As the name indicates, these specific annuities are LINKED TO, NOT IN an index. By far the most common index is the S&P 500 index. When the index makes a gain over a 12 month period, you also receive a gain up to whatever the cap of the annuity is set at. For instance, the annuity may have a cap of 7%. Next year it may be 6.5% or 8%. If the S&P 500 returns 10%, you get everything up to you cap like the 7% example.

But if the S&P 500 goes south and gives a negative return of ANY amount, you are fully protected from loss. Nice. IMPORTANT: The new LOWER level of the index is your new starting point for gains next year. If you buy the annuity when the S&P 500 is at 1000 and next year it is down to 900, you don't gain, but you also don't lose. However, the annuity resets to 900. So year two it raises to 990, it just gained 10% and you receive all of it up to your cap, even though you're not even back to where the index started when you bought it.

If you choose this annuity, you can actually have and access your funds, and the gains, without having to die! This is a big deal if you're in retirement. You won't get this feature in a variable annuity UNLESS you actually do have a gain, and those "conditions" let you have the money! This is where people get mixed up. They remember the rep telling them about the guarantee and think they have a gain when actually they have a loss. It's shameful.

Single Premium Immediate Annuities: These annuities have their place and may be self explanatory, but let's make sure shall we. Your part is to deposit one lump sum into the annuity. Their part (the insurance company) is to pay you an income for the rest of your life. The amount of income is based on several things:

1. How old you are.
2. How long the IRS mortality table says you're going to live.
3. How much money you put into the annuity.
4. Whether you are male or female.
5. How you want to be paid.

   Life only

   Life with 10, 15, 20 year certain

   5,10,15 years

   A certain percentage per year

   A certain dollar amount per year

Life only pays the highest amount compared to Life with Period Certain, BUT if you die two years later, the insurance company keeps the balance. That's why so many people choose life WITH a guaranteed payout period in case you die prematurely.

The next choice isn't for life, just a period of time. The shorter the time period, the higher the payout, because the balance must be zero when it expires.

Lastly, you can just tell the company that you want a certain percentage or a certain dollar amount until the annuity runs out.

Common Denominators of Annuities

All three annuities, except the Single Premium annuity, described above have some common rules and benefits. Any annuity worth having offers a free 10% per year withdrawal feature. They let you have some limited access to your money without incurring a penalty or fee for getting it. If you need more than 10% of the balance in a 12 month period, there may be a fee or partial surrender charge applied.

Another thing they share is what happens when you do take money out on an 'every so often' kind of system. Remember what I said earlier in the chapter? The insurance company must give you gains first. Are the gains taxable? Yes, they are.

A variation of taking money out haphazardly, is taking it out on a scheduled program as I described above. The advantage of taking money this way is that the insurance company gives you a combination of gains and your deposited money at the same time. An exemption percentage applies to your withdrawal. It means that a portion of your withdrawal is exempt from taxes because it was your money to begin with. Understand?

IRA's. All these annuity choices can also be an IRA. You won't gain any tax advantage by doing it. Both have the 59½ rule and 10% early withdrawal penalty. Both are tax deferred and taxed at income rates coming back out. So why do it? Because the fixed and indexed annuity choices are safe! Because you're tired and fed up with losing money in the funds you have them in.

Overall, I like safe annuities and I really, really like the indexed annuity. **BUT** they still cannot compete against the indexed life insurance policy since they are tax free and pay higher returns. Now, ever think about buying an investment property? Read the next chapter first!

Investment Properties

Mom taught me how to investigate, "Would you just look at that dirt on the back of your neck?"

"Well, since I'm not an owl and I don't have a mirror, then no." See, now that's not the best, most respectful response I could have said to my mom. I learned other things about moms that day. Did you know that they can be very quick when they want to be? Wow! In case you are wondering what the dirt on the back of your neck, has to do with this chapter, I'm illustrating how you need to know about things that aren't readily seen or known. If you decide that having an investment property is an option for you, then look for the "dirt behind the neck". Look for the expenses, the problems, the issues that are not easily seen. You have to dig!

When you are considering a single family dwelling, a duplex, a fourplex, an apartment building, commercial building or something else, you'll be surprised at the amount of dirt behind the neck. Owners don't want you to know where the dirt is (the facts) because the more you know, the more you can negotiate, which costs them money.

In today's depressed real estate environment (and future ones for that matter), there are lots of folks out there that are trying to take advantage of low prices and low mortgage rates. The media talks about all the deals out there and how it's a great time to buy. Do those same media people go the extra mile and tell you what to watch out for beyond the common sense stuff that's obvious? No. They can't because they don't know themselves. Don't worry, I've got your back. Here are some important things to look for.

What to look for #1 – Financial Statements

I'm amazed at how many clients have brought in financial statements from a potential investment property and how ready they were to sign, just off those statements. Here's what you should see as a bare minimum.

Get the last *three years of financial statements* detailing the operations of the property. Make sure they are SIGNED!! It will stand up in court if push comes to shove. If they won't sign them, red flags should come shooting out of every orifice of your body. Don't go there! It's just a metaphor.

Next, you need a *current budget*. This will give you a better idea of the spending habits of the current management. If you can improve on them, it translates to cash flow.

Get a *current revenue* report. The budget and revenue reports will give you the details that the financial statement generalizes. You need to know where all the revenue sources are so again, you can get a better picture of opportunities.

Another important report is the *collections report*. Wouldn't you want to know how often non-payment comes up? By who? How difficult it is to get it and the cost involved? I would.

Likewise, you'll want a *vacancy report*. What is the ratio? Is it seasonally related, or just bad management or pricing? You better know it historically. Talk about having an impact on revenue.

Closely related to the vacancy report is the *rent history*. What are the comparable rents going for around town? Are you high, low or just right? How long has it been since there was a rent increase? Can you justify one when you take over? Will it force out the bad apples? These are good documents to start with. Get them!

What to look for #2 – Expenses

If you get through the financial documents and you are comfortable with them from a revenue point of view, now focus on expenses. Not in general off the main financial statement, but in detail as above.

Property taxes. What are they? Can they be lowered in some sort of negotiation? Are they just too high and no one has ever bothered to go to the city and say so? What are the chances of them raising in the next few years? Cash flow people.

Insurances. You would be wise to get the insurance statements, ALL insurances, for the last three years. It will give you a peek at how the prices have been running. Probably increasing, but you may be pleasantly surprised. Don't count on it though.

Equipment leases. Is the copier on a lease? How about the vehicles if any? How much time is left on the lease and will it pass with the property? If not, that may even be a blessing in disguise.

Staff salaries. How much are they being paid? Is it a contract? What, if any, are the other benefits they receive?

Lawn care and snow removal. Does management have a contract with a company to provide this service or do they do it? How much is it a season? Is it a contracted bid? When does it expire so you can put out for bid again?

Security service. Is the building in a secured community? Is the security electronic? Are there real security people? Both? Can the service be negotiated, or even terminated?

Management service. Is the property being run by a management company? What's the percentage they require? Can that be renegotiated or tiered based on performance? The higher the rents per quarter, the better the percentage they get. The reverse would also be true. Where does their responsibility stop and yours start? How long is the contract for?

Utilities. You would do well to get three years worth of these too. You want to see the trends for the phones, heat, electric, propane, garbage, water, cable, and so on.

Maintenance. This one is important because it could be an indicator of serious costs in the near future. Get the details of any maintenance performed for the building, the mechanical system, the electrical system, the phone system, the plumbing, parking lot, sprinkler system and everything else you can think of guys. Why? If you need to have something re-done, there may be warranties, there may be a law suit, who knows. With this disclosure, get any insurance claims that have been made against the owners, the property or anything else. You need to know what you're getting into!

Marketing. Do the owners advertise? How? Do they use the radio or TV or the paper? Is it necessary? Take a look at your vacancy ratio and you'll know. Is there a waiting list? Why or why not. If something is working, identify it and keep it. If something isn't working, AND it's costing you, get rid of it.

What to look for #3 – Existing Rental Agreements

Get a copy of the rental agreement the renters actually get and sign. Do you agree with it? Are there things in it that handcuff you? Are there old, outdated lease agreements floating around that need to be dealt with?

How much are the rental deposits for each type of unit? A two bedroom deposit versus a three bedroom for example. Now catch this, you ready? MAKE SURE THE DEPOSIT MONEY TRANSFERS WITH THE PURCHASE! This one is missed all the time. That money is supposed to be tracked and held for refunds. Get it!

Get a copy of the rent roll. You will want the history of each renter to see what their pay history is like. Who's constantly late versus on time, versus collections and when was the last time they had a rent increase?

You also have the right to know what the credit reports are of all these people. Again, you want to know what you're getting into!

What to look for #4 – Inventory

It's pretty simple. Get a list of all the stuff that comes with the property, or should come with the property.

Office equipment. Things like the copier, the phones, computers. Also the office supplies. It adds up in a hurry and when you're just getting going, you are watching every penny. You should be anyway.

Appliances. What things are included here? Stoves, refrigerators, heaters and AC units should be obvious. HOWEVER, what about replacement appliances of all those things, and other things as well? Toilets, water heaters, paint, carpet and so forth.

Grounds equipment. Are there mowers, snow blowers, trimmers, pruners, trucks, trailers and other equipment that are essential to the upkeep of the property?

Tools and out buildings. Surely there are basic hand tools and maybe special tools needed to work on specific equipment. Have you priced tools lately? It adds up in a hurry. Where are all the tools, the rakes, shovels, trimmers, gas cans and trash cans stored? Are you getting those? Write it down? The buildings and sheds should come with the purchase but don't assume it.

What to look for #5 – Property Condition & Appearance

Are the *units furnished or unfurnished*? If they are furnished, how worn out is the furniture? Is there an inventory list? If items have been stolen or destroyed, who is going to pay for the replacement of those items? If you have to replace it, get a discount on the purchase price. Then, go after the renters to recover.

Cleanliness. Are the apartments, condos, homes etc. astatically clean? Do they smell like smoke, or pets, or moldy?

Size. How many square feet are the units? What's the cost per square foot? How does that cost compare with the market? You can go to the Chamber of Commerce, a local realtor or the builders association to get a feel for the market.

Up to date. Whatever the physical condition of the above things, are those things outdated? If so, it has a mental affect on people thinking about renting from you. When the carpets, the tile, the counters, the fixtures or the appliances are something out of the '70's, you can't charge as much.

Location. Where are the units built? Is the area in a market that's going downhill? Is it heading in an upward trend? What's the crime rate like? Are schools close by? Is it close to a business district? How about parks? What about the scenery? Is it facing a mountain range or lake or golf course? It affects the price.

Amenities. Consider what amenities the property comes with vs. what it could have. Keep it to yourself because this is an area where you can increase revenue.

Clubhouse. If it has a clubhouse, what's the condition of it and how often is it used? If not, could putting one up and charging for it, be an option.

Pool. Is there a pool? Is it safe? Is it expensive? So, is it necessary?

Vending. Is there coin laundry available? How about soda and candy or chip machines? There are lots of things that can be put in a vending machine these days. Be observant and find a need and then fill it.

Miscellaneous. How about covered parking? Better yet, are there garages with power? Tennis or volleyball or basketball courts set you apart as well.

What to look for #6 – Financing and Legal Docs

Let's assume for a moment that ALL the issues I brought up have passed your inspection and you are ready to move on this opportunity, now how will you go about buying it?

Financing options. Compare the options with each other. You are looking for the best CASH FLOW option. Translation, pick the one giving you the lowest payment. You have 30 year loans, ARM's, and don't forget the owner themselves. What would a contract for deed look like? What about a lease with an option to buy? Hear me on this one because it's effective. You ready?

I would gladly pay whatever the owner wants for a property IF I GET TO STATE THE TERMS! Find a balance between these two things and you have a home run.

Taxes. To be safe and to protect yourself, it would be prudent to check that the taxes are up to date. Also check whether there are potential tax increases that could go into effect.

Liens. I know, you're thinking that any liens would come out on the clear title check, right? Well, it should, but stranger things have happened. Like pending liens and lawsuits, for example. Mechanics liens are not an uncommon lien and if they are pending, they might go unnoticed on a title check.

Zoning & building codes. Are any codes being violated because they came into existence AFTER the current owners bought the property? If so, are you going to need to upgrade something when it changes ownership? That could be expensive, so you check into it yourself, ok? Don't take the owners word for it.

Ordinances. Some cities or counties have rent control ordinances. Does one apply where this property is located? It will limit your rents so find out.

Past Due accounts. Lastly, you should know whether or not the owners are current on all their utilities, loans, leases and other obligations.

Investing in property can make you wealthy, but, if done wrong or in a naïve way, it can cause you to drool uncontrollably by yourself in corner somewhere. The kids will be fitting you for a straight jacket and looking for a good home that will accept you. Just be smart about it and good luck!

Now let's keep your identity safe. Turn the page and keep reading.

Identity Theft: Keep your assets along with your sanity

Mom taught me about organization, "Clean up this room or so help me I'm gonna knock you into the middle of next week!"

It's amazing what a little bit of intimidation does for a young child. Now don't get the wrong impression about my mom. I'm just using lines that lots of families used back in the olden-days, and most of us still turned out just fine.

So what is it exactly that people who steal our identities want from us? That's an easy question right? They want our money, our credit, basically, they want access to our "stuff". Now, what do these people need from us in order to get our stuff? They will gladly take your Social Security number, your date of birth, your driver's license number. They will try to get your passwords, your pin numbers, your mother's maiden name, your pet's names, your phone numbers and address. The brass ring, sort-a-speak, would be your account numbers for anything with money in them.

That's why all the above mentioned items are things you should protect with all the effort you can muster. If you have ever gone through the process of fixing or repairing your credit, retrieving money or assets someone stole from you, or protecting whatever assets you still have, then you know about the stress and the huge inconvenience it is to get your life back.

I have a son and a sister that have both had their identity stolen. In my son's case, he didn't lose anything! We visit our accounts by habit, on a daily basis. One day online, there it was, a transaction that was completely out of character. We made a call to the bank, and sure enough, it was originated somewhere in Spain. I have to give a big high five to Wells Fargo's fraud detection department on this because it was caught and shut down so quickly that no money was finalized in a transfer. It turned out that somehow this person found out about my son's password on a Pay Pal account. Now listen closely, it WAS NOT Pay Pal that messed up, it was just one of those things. We'll never know how he got it, but he was caught and that's the main thing.

How Your Identity Can Be Stolen

In The Home

People forget about this, but taking mail out of your mailbox is so easy and quick, no wonder it's a favorite among thieves. Even though it is a federal offense, they have to be caught doing it. Who watches their mailbox all day? I suppose a person could hook up a cheap video camera. Some people install locking mailboxes, which is cheaper than the video route. One thing is for sure, you should keep track of your mail! Buy a good shredder and anything you receive that has personal information on it, you should shred if you don't need it. Including, opening your junk mail. Yes, it's a pain, but identity theft is more of a pain. Be aware of people that come to your home for service work.

People like contractors or repairman and maids or salesman can see mail that you left on your kitchen table.

Take opened mail that you need and put it out of sight when you have company come over. I know how badly we want to trust people, but in today's world, you just can't blindly live your life. You and I both have heard of the stories out there where people they trusted are the ones that have hurt them the most. Keep track of old pay stubs, old bills, cancelled checks, statements, all those kinds of things, and file them away somewhere.

If you have elderly parents or siblings, they are especially vulnerable to phone type scams. Educate them how dangerous it is to give information over the phone. You are doing them and yourself a favor.

In Public

I took my family to Spain in June 2010. It was a great, uneventful trip, FOR US, not for someone else in the group. One day when we were visiting a bull fighting museum, one of our ladies set her camera down right next to her on a stone pillar so she could grab something else. There were four to five high school kids from our group right there with her. Low and behold a young Spanish youth comes by and snatches the camera. Well, that was a mistake because two of our guys were on the track team and they took off after him. Just before catching him, the guy dropped the camera and gets away. It was in its case, so it wasn't damaged at all. Oh wait, you probably don't care about that.

That's an interesting story, Shawn, but what's the point? While in the states, we were warned over and over about how bold and talented the pickpockets were in Spain. They are numerous, organized, and experienced. We landed in Rome and our guide starts right in with the same message. Hmm, seems to be a pattern here. I guess we better sit up and take notice.

Identity theft is at an all time high. In 2009 there were over 1.3 million identity thefts in America, and we have surpassed that number in 2010. People are desperate and willing to risk jail and fines in exchange for your "stuff".

I don't want you to panic, I just want you to know that people are watching you more than you think. If they see an opportunity, like that Spanish youth did, they might take a chance. Eliminate the temptation by being aware of your surroundings and your wallet, purses, and things of value. If you get lazy, then don't be surprised if you become a target.

At Work

Theft has always been a problem for employers. That's nothing new, but, even more now than ever, theft is coming from the employees against the employer AND other employees. So here's what you do. Don't walk away from your purse or wallet unless you have it locked in a drawer or locker. Others will get your various forms of ID and quickly run them over to a copier to get the information off them. They will return them and you have no idea it even took place.

Another area in the work place that can be a breeding ground for illegal acts is the HR department. This is where your employee files are most likely kept. Depending on the size of your company, there may not be an HR department, which means your employee file is even more accessible to people of low character. It means your file may be in a common file drawer in a mid level managers office that doesn't think to lock the office door. IF they even have a door. Think about what's in your employee file for a second. Everything a thief needs to steal your identity is there on a silver platter. What do we do with the good silver people? That's right, we lock it up. So make sure that the people who have your file keep it safe, and don't disclose information about you to every John Doe that asks for it.

On The Internet

If you recall the story I shared about my son, this is the way that he was compromised. Electronically stealing assets and identities is the scariest because it is so fast and devastating at the same time.

Spyware, also known as "key loggers", is a software virus that embeds itself into websites you visit. It also embeds itself on to your personal computer. Then, it records your keystrokes. The people behind this awful software can now get into any account you open, or already have established somewhere, plus any card information you disclose while buying something online. An account you check on, like your online banking account is obviously vulnerable too.

Fraudware. This is a sneaky little sucker. It is a software virus that masquerades as a legitimate virus protection program. Then, while online it will come up in a window claiming to have caught multiple virus attacks. It tells you about MANY attacks, usually dozens if not more than one hundred, which is one way you know it's this virus. Here comes the "gotcha" part of the scam. It will then tell you that your virus software is not activated so you can't delete or fix the barrage of viruses you are being hit with. There will be a link, or instruction to click on the window to activate your virus software, (which ASKS FOR YOUR CREDIT CARD INFO). If you recognize and catch this scam, it's one of the easiest viruses to remove, especially when you have a legitimate virus protection software program, already on your computer.

Phishing. These are e-mails you have probably received before. These e-mails tell you that an account you created has expired, or someone else has attempted to access your account. Then the e-mail instructs you to validate your account by confirming your username and password and then click reply. DON'T DO IT!! The very bold scammers will even try to find the born suckers that will give them their Social Security number. NO LEGITIMATE website will EVER ask you to validate your login information. They already have it.

Wireless Networks. When you have a wireless network in your home, you need to make sure it is encrypted. WHY? A neighbor or someone parked on the street, for crying out loud, can access your network and see everything you're doing. Are you ok with that? I hope not. The same thing applies for your small business. If you, or your business, have any wealth at all, there are people that can get on to your unprotected network and use a program called "packet sniffers" that do the same thing as Spyware above, only remotely. So what do you do? Protect your network.

As a recap, here is a short list of things you can do to protect yourself from this threat:

- Use a locking mailbox. Take important mail to the post office yourself
- Consider getting a PO Box
- Don't leave mail laying around when you have company
- Buy yourself a good shredder that can handle credit cards. Shred cards, old bills, old statements, old applications, cancelled checks, junk mail with your information on it
- Only use a "Gel Pen" when signing checks. The ink doesn't work for "check washing" where the payee is erased and filled in again
- Run a strong magnet over the magnetic strip of old credit cards and drivers licenses
- Consider a credit monitoring service if you are wealthy or a high profile person
- Password protect your computers at home and at work
- Password protect your wireless networks wherever they are located
- Password protect your individual accounts and make it different from your other logins
- Don't carry your Social Security card, your birth certificate, passports, all your credit cards and forms of ID unless you REALLY need to
- Be aware of who's around you in public. Protect line of site at the checkout and ATM machines

I hope with all my heart that someone does not steal your identity. If you will follow these simple steps, the likelihood of it happening will be drastically reduced, but not eliminated.

If it does happen, be proactive and shut down everything you can right away to contain and limit the damage. Something I did years ago and have always updated ever since, is I created a secure master file where I have every account number, password, user name, PIN number, website, ID number, you name it, in a set of individual files. I separate them by topic, like all banking information is on one file, all website logins are another, general information like SSN's, DL's, Passport #'s and such are another file. My Wills and trusts and insurances are another file. All of my business information and licenses get their own file.

Whatever you have of value that you want to protect and access at a moment's notice, you may want to do the same thing. I have a duplicate of all this information on a thumb drive so I have access to the information no matter where I am. It's great and I hope you do the same thing.

You are just about done with this book. Read my closing thoughts and then take action on what you have learned.

Closing Thoughts

Mom taught me about wisdom, "Lending money to friends creates amnesia."

I've had a wonderful time writing this book. The topic of money can be either controversial or freeing, depending on how you have managed your money and certain conditions beyond your control. Your comfort level with the topic of money will be directly related to your "Financial Literacy". Will you be the one squirming when the conversation goes in a certain direction, or the one setting people straight (respectfully, of course).

As I said earlier in the book, I hope you take this information to heart and act on what I gave you. It will change your life for the better. It could change the lives of your kids, your friends, siblings, parents, anyone. Tell them what you learned. Suggest they go get this book, or give one as a gift to them.

I hope I kept my promise to keep this book as short as I can without stealing from you. I tried to make it entertaining to some degree so you wouldn't slip into a coma mid-way through. You have been given a glimpse into what I take very seriously and have a strong passion about.

I still do public seminars to educate people in areas they have no idea about, but can harm them in ways that are beyond repair. For now, I still take clients from all around the country. However, I still speak with people that have been given all the tools, all the strategies, and all the education they need to take action, but amazingly still say no. Please, for the love of all that's good, don't be one of these people.

Dads and husbands, listen up. If you take care of the finances in your home because you think that you can do a better job or you think women are the weaker sex and can't or shouldn't handle it, first shame on you. Second, here's a news flash for you: if you think women are the weaker sex, just try pulling the blankets back to your side. Seriously, maybe you are the right choice, but based on years of meeting with couples, you probably are not. Women are GENERALLY wired to get this stuff better than us. Swallow your pride and let her try.

Moms and wives, it's time to take an interest in what's going on in the financial world. I see one or the other of the following couples. Either the wife is 100% disinterested in anything pertaining to their homes financial health that it's scary, OR they take 100% control of everything and almost insult the husband in front of me about how inept they are. Neither way is beneficial. You are supposed to be a team. Help each other, encourage each other, and find out how great it is to be prepared for the unexpected events life tends to throw at us when we're not looking.

I'm not so out of touch as to believe that everyone who reads this book is going to actually do something about their life. I know that I shouldn't expect an 11 X 14 idea to be accepted by a 2 X 4 mind. But for those of you who do get what I'm trying to teach you, and believe that what I'm saying is true, be prepared for some serious, life changing benefits.

Life is a gift. It isn't something that we earned, or created. It isn't something we totally control or sustain. One thing we often forget is that we are all going to die, and the other thing we forget is that we are alive! So, do what you can to make your life and the lives of your loved ones, better, safer, wealthier, happier and protected. Remember, the man on top of the mountain didn't just fall there. God Bless.

Other Products From Solomon Group, LLC

- **Double sided $2 Bill Puzzle. Magnetic version.** Use this very visual, fun, concept puzzle for group presentations. It's a four piece puzzle on one side, but a five piece puzzle on the other side. Large enough to see from the back of the room. When a volunteer comes up to put the four sided puzzle together, it looks complete. Have them sit down and you remove the puzzle and put it back up the other way around. Now, the presidents head is gone. You have the "missing piece" in your pocket, because YOU, Your Company, Your Product, ARE the missing piece they need. Powerful! $24.95

- Double sided $2 Bill Puzzle. Desktop Version. Just like the magnetic version but meant for one-on-one consultations. Use on a desk, tabletop or any flat surface. $14.95

Ordering information: Call 832-38-PIECE

To find out how Solomon Group or Shawn Williams can help you, call 832-38-PIECE or e-mail Solomon Group at: Solomon@smig.net

www.ingramcontent.com/pod-product-compliance
Lightning Source LLC
Chambersburg PA
CBHW060621210326
41520CB00010B/1419